SERENITY
MEDITATION™ SERIES

A NEW BEGINNING

Samaritan Counseling Center

THOMAS NELSON PUBLISHERS
Nashville

Why a New Beginning?

We live in a sexually preoccupied society. Sex is everywhere. It's talked about, written about, joked about, and paraded about to sell everything from cars and soap to fashion and food. It's the advertising by-line that grabs attention, and so much so it has now become part of the American dream—meaning more sex, better sex, different sex, or even more, better, and different partners is what life is really all about.

But our passion for sexual knowledge and experience is not making us more caring, compassionate lovers. Instead, it is causing more dissatisfaction, dysfunction, and abuse. Beneath this veneer of smiling sexual glitter lies a generation of sexually wounded women:

- One out of ten women admits to having been raped.

- This year over one million children will be sexually abused.

- Thirty million adult women have been sexually wounded through abuse.

And this is just the tip of the iceberg! Every day we hear more about sexual violation, dysfunction, and harassment.

My profound concern is for the wounded hearts that carry the pain of all this sin. Both the innocent and not-so-innocent will live lives of grief until the wounds are healed and the memories cleansed.

Sexual wounding can be devastating for a woman. It strikes at the very core of who she is, violating the intimate boundaries of her person. When sex and sexy bodies are used to advertise the American ideal, it further denigrates who she is and compounds what has happened to her. It causes confusion, insecurity, shame, and pain, making it extremely hard for her to embrace the pleasure and sacredness of sex that God intended. Recovery is needed.

But recovery is not an event, it's a process. Healing takes time, support, and understanding. It also takes God. Sexual wounds are deep wounds of the spirit. They require the deep and sensitive work of God's Holy Spirit. More than one woman in counseling has stated "if only there were a daily prayer or devotional I could use to help me heal. God sometimes seems so far off." Others have become angry with God, wondering why He didn't prevent their abuse. All need to experience Him in order to heal.

This devotional is our love offering to the many women who are struggling with their pain and shame and want to experience God in it. We are confident that He will not abandon or disappoint you. It is our prayer that as each of you face your wounds and face God with them, healing will come. When sex becomes painful and shame makes you cower, He is near. It is His touch that is available to remove the harm, heal the hurts, and give you *a new beginning.*

Alfred Ells

This devotional is a collaborative effort born of our desire to bless women who have been sexually abused. René Mummert has been our ever faithful word processor and assistant. Her organizational skills and extra effort made it easier for all. The art work has come from Karen Thompson's creative pen. And Carlene Hacker has touched all of us with her heart-wrenching poetry. Jane Jones from Thomas Nelson has added invaluable encouragement and expertise. She was always there when we needed her. My wife, Susan, as usual, has helped do everything.

As staff members and friends of Samaritan Counseling Services, we want to thank the Board of Directors and other employees for their support and prayers.

Most of all we want to thank Jesus for allowing us the opportunity to comfort others with the comfort He has given us (2 Cor. 1:3, 4 NIV).

Christy Edison Behymer	Karen Caudill
René Diamond	Susan Ells
Kerstin Fowler	Chris Midyett
Linda Muir	René Mummert
Edye Ruoho	Susan Syfert
Karen Thompson	Catherine St. James
Sandra Johnson	Alfred Ells

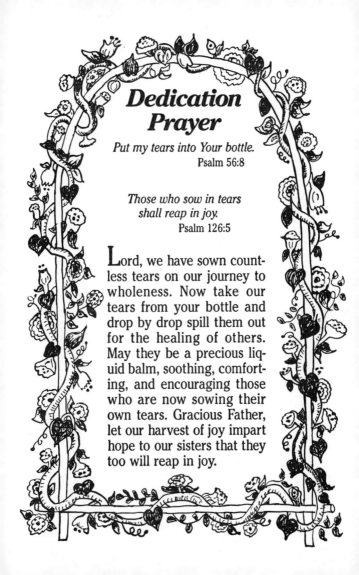

Dedication Prayer

Put my tears into Your bottle.
Psalm 56:8

*Those who sow in tears
shall reap in joy.*
Psalm 126:5

Lord, we have sown countless tears on our journey to wholeness. Now take our tears from your bottle and drop by drop spill them out for the healing of others. May they be a precious liquid balm, soothing, comforting, and encouraging those who are now sowing their own tears. Gracious Father, let our harvest of joy impart hope to our sisters that they too will reap in joy.

A NEW BEGINNING

The morning sunlight
slides through my window,
awakening this day and me.
Looking out at my world,
I see millions of laughing leaves,
shimmering and dancing
in the playful breeze,
mirroring the delight,
the calm within my soul.

This is a new day.
The war is over,
the weapons thrown along
the long, rough path toward home.
Once immovable monuments
in my mind,
now old battle scenes
appear as distant mirages,
and the Son's smile
warms my heart.

© Carlene Hacker

Behold, I will do a new thing;
Now it shall spring forth;
Shall you not know it?
I will even make a road in
  the wilderness
And rivers in the desert.

Isaiah 43:19

Today is the beginning of a new year. With each new year more of God's plan unfolds for us. This year does not have to be like all of the others. In Him, we have hope. In Him, we have healing. In Him, we have the promise that the shame of our youth will be forgotten (Isa. 54:4). In Him, we have forgiveness—forgiveness for ourselves and for those who abused and wounded us.

Take heart! God is not ignorant of our pain. A new thing shall spring forth for you. Look for it and He will show it to you.

Lord, help me to embrace this new year as a year of hope and healing.

Ah, Lord God! Behold, You have made the heavens and the earth by Your great power and outstretched arm. There is nothing too hard for You.
Jeremiah 32:17

How big is your God? Is He the God who made the heavens and the earth with His great power, or have you confined Him in a box, limiting His ability to work in your life?

Let Him out! Allow God to demonstrate His power and creativity. God is bigger than anything you are going through.

Lord, may I never close You up in a box. Let me allow You to demonstrate Your great power in my life, trusting always that nothing is too hard for You.

*This also comes from the LORD
  of hosts,
Who is wonderful in counsel and
  excellent in guidance.*
                                    Isaiah 28:29

The nineties! The age of self-help and how-to books, tapes, videos, and magazines. Everyone is in search of beauty, knowledge, success, and fulfillment. Those of us who have suffered from sexual abuse feel an even greater need for answers and help.

STOP. Listen to the Lord of hosts, our Creator, the One who really knows us because He created us. He has a specific purpose for each of our lives and He wants us to look to Him for counsel and guidance.

Open your heart and mind to Him. Allow His wisdom to penetrate through Scripture, prayer, and godly people. Look to the Lord of hosts for guidance. You will stand back in awe and amazement as He works.

_____

Father, help me to look to You, not to the world, for wise counsel and guidance.

And prove me now in this . . .
If I will not open for you the windows
* of heaven*
And pour out for you such blessing
That there will not be room enough
*   to receive it.*   Malachi 3:10

Our heavenly Father wants to fill our lives with His blessings. We need to open our hands and release everything to Him so that He might remove those things that hinder.

The dilemma is that we usually grasp what is ours too tightly, the good and the bad. We fear being stripped naked. It takes faith and trust in a loving heavenly Father to completely let go. We must remember that He will give us new things after we let go of the old. He will not leave us naked, ashamed, or neglected. He will glorify Himself in miraculous ways by filling our lives with His blessing.

Lord, I open my hands and my life to you. Remove everything that does not belong and pour out Your blessings.

My times are in Your hand.
Psalm 31:15

Never think that God's delays are God's denials. His timing is not our timing, but it is always perfect. We become impatient to see changes in ourselves, others, or situations in our lives, but our heavenly Father knows all that must be done in people's hearts. He knows what circumstances need to be before we can see something tangible.

Many times, in my anguish and pain, I have cried out to the Lord, "Father, nothing is happening! Where are You? Why are You not doing something?" Then I sense Him saying, "You may not see anything happening, my child, but I am working. Trust me." With this reassurance in my heart, I can go on a little longer.

Lord, help me to remember that my life is in Your hands and that Your timing is perfect. Help me to trust even when I don't see the answer.

> *But now, thus says the LORD, who created*
>   *you, O Jacob,*
> *And He who formed you, O Israel:*
> *"Fear not, for I have redeemed you;*
> *I have called you by your name;*
> *You are Mine."*
>   Isaiah 43:1

Scripture says God created the nation of Israel for Himself. Even though the people of Israel suffered because of their own sins and the sins of others against them, God still claimed they were His.

Sometimes we wonder who we belong to and question who really cares about us. But our Lord tells us that He formed and created each of us. We are not to be afraid, for no matter what happens to us He will redeem us. Because He calls me by name, I have a purpose. I have security and I belong. I AM HIS!

———————

Thank You, Lord Jesus, for redeeming me and claiming me as Your own in spite of my sins and the sins of others against me.

*The Spirit of God has made me, and the breath
of the Almighty gives me life.*   Job 33:4

The most important part of our recovery from sexual abuse is learning who we are in the Lord. As we
begin to heal, we may find that we are nothing like
people have told us all our lives. We may find that
we *aren't* angry or that we *aren't* shy, backward,
ashamed, ugly, lazy, or even passive. When we strip
away all the lies that we have believed about our
identities, we may feel like empty shells. We may
feel even worse than before.

Let us ask the Creator, the One who made us,
who knows us best and gives us life, to fill in the
blanks. "Who am I, Lord?" can be the most exciting
question we've ever asked.

---

*Thank You, Lord, for making me and giving me life. You know
what You made me to be. Teach me who I am.*

*And do not be conformed to this world, but be
transformed by the renewing of your mind,
that you may prove what is that good and
acceptable and perfect will of God.*

Romans 12:2

I held the Transformer toy in my hand, changing
the car into a robot and then back again. I wondered what I would be changed into when Jesus got
through with me. I had spent my whole life trying to
please people; I was a robot that would be whatever
others wanted. Now Jesus wanted me to be the person He had made.

Being transformed into a new creature can be
scary and unsettling. What will I enjoy doing? What
purpose will I have? Whatever happens, I know the
Holy Spirit will take care of everything. He just asks
that we make ourselves available to Him, trusting in
the good things He has revealed about Himself. He
will adjust our thinking, transforming us into the
new persons we need to be.

*Lord, renew my mind so that I may do what is Your good, perfect,
and acceptable will.*

For I know the thoughts that I think toward you,
says the LORD, thoughts of peace and not of
evil, to give you a future and a hope.

Jeremiah 29:11

In all the pain and confusion of my childhood, somehow I got the impression that God was out to get me. I thought all the bad things that happened to me were His way of getting even with me for having been so bad.

I have come to understand that it was not in God's plan for me to be abused and hurt as a child. In fact, I believe that God's heart hurts just as mine does over the horrible acts that took place.

God is not going to hurt me. He actually wants good things for me!

It helps to know that God wants to give me hope for my future. My job is to know God as He truly is and trust His plans for my life.

God, help me to believe that You have good things in store for me.

*And you shall know the truth, and the truth
shall make you free.*
John 8:32

When people told me I was pretty, smart, or gifted,
I'd thank them and walk away in disbelief. Although
their words were very kind, I was sure they were
just nice words. I believed I was inadequate. I felt
tainted by the abuse. I knew I couldn't measure up
to others.

One day I met a woman who was very artistic. I
told her how beautiful her work was. She smiled,
but she said, "It isn't very good." Suddenly I realized
that I had responded like that many times in my
own life. Her response made me realize I had believed a lie—that I was not good enough. But the
truth is that in Jesus I am good enough. He accepts
me.

_____

*Lord, I am acceptable in Your sight. Help me to accept the gifts
You've given me.*

But by the grace of God I am what I am.
1 Corinthians 15:10

Learning love for self seems to be the most difficult process for those of us who have been abused. The Lord wants to help us discover ourselves—who He created us to be.

As we love and accept ourselves, love for others begins to manifest itself within us. Our joy for life reaches new heights as we love Christ, and we find the peace for which we have searched so long.

We need to surrender our distorted self-images to God so that He can begin the process of renewing our minds through His grace.

Dear God, thank You for guiding me in the process of self-discovery and bringing me to self-acceptance so that I can honestly say, "I'm glad that I am what I am."

> *Behold, this Child is destined.*
> Luke 2:34

These words were spoken about Jesus, but in the Father's mind every child has a destiny. For those of us who have suffered rejection, abandonment, and abuse, it is difficult to realize that God has always had a purpose for our lives.

As I struggled with the concept of my identity and destiny I felt that God shared this with me.

You are a daughter of destiny uniquely gifted to fill a place in My kingdom no one else can fill. Know that my love and mercy are extended to you and that my desire is for you to find your identity and fulfillment in Me. Today resolve in your heart to explore your destiny by stopping the self-condemnation that has kept you from seeking Me.

Today, Lord, I repent of the judgments I have made against myself. Help me embrace the destiny You have for me.

*But we have renounced the hidden things
of shame, not walking in craftiness nor
handling the word of God deceitfully, but
by manifestation of the truth commending
ourselves to every man's conscience in the
sight of God.*
2 Corinthians 4:2

The apostle Paul was subjected to every kind of human weakness, persecution, and suffering, yet he did not resort to dishonesty, craftiness, or deceit. Paul knew that God is truth and that harboring secret thoughts, feelings, or desires only destroys the truth God wants revealed.

And so it is in our day. Any manipulation or dishonesty on our part only delays God's straight arrows of truth that would pierce our hearts. We can choose to renounce the hidden shameful things and bring to light the truth.

*Lord, today I renounce my hidden things of shame. Help me
share Your truth.*

Why are you cast down, O my soul?
And why are you disquieted within me?
Hope in God.
                                        Psalm 42:11

There were feelings stirring deep within me that I wasn't used to feeling and didn't understand. Why was I so unsettled, so disturbed?

I had constructed a closet for all my feelings and kept its door shut, so God and others wouldn't know all the secrets hidden within me. Now the door was opening.

God was showing me my need and His desire to heal every part of my life. Inch by inch I began to open the door. As I did, He told me He loved me no matter what and healed each new feeling I gave Him. As my hope and trust in Him grew, I realized God had already known about my closet, but had waited patiently for me to let Him help.

Thank You, Lord, for being patient and for giving me hope. Help me to always turn to You when I am downcast and troubled.

"Not by might, nor by power, but by My Spirit"
says the Lord of Hosts.   Zechariah 4:6

Hopeless
Helpless
Powerless
Am I

These feelings are written on the heart of every woman who has suffered the overwhelming pain of abuse. They resurface when she faces the painful memories of those dark years.

Today, as I feel the feelings while examining the past, one thing is very different. Now I have a strength I did not have then. Jesus is in me and I am in Him. I can face anything without fear, even the painful memories. I can look at them and deal with them—not by my power, but by the power of His Spirit working within me.

Lord, I surrender my feelings of hopelessness, helplessness, and powerlessness to Your Holy Spirit.

I will give you the treasures of darkness
And hidden riches of secret places.

Isaiah 45:3

As I pondered this passage in my quiet time, thinking it was perhaps for someone else, God impressed on me that it really was for me. Just what did it mean? "Secret places" to me represented places of sin. How could I ever forget or forgive myself for that secret sin? I was so fearful of its being uncovered and brought into the open. I had so much to lose if the truth were known. His conviction helped me overcome my fear. I finally prayed, "Lord, enter into my darkness and bring my secret sin to light."

Since that fearful day, the Lord has forgiven me, erased the guilt, and restored my life. Instead of the loss I expected, my life has been incredibly enriched. He exchanged His treasures and hidden riches—healing, peace, and joy—for my secret shame and sin.

Lord, exchange my darkness and secret sin for Your treasures and rich blessings.

Then I would not be ashamed,
When I look into all Your
commandments.

Psalm 119:6

Shame can keep a person bound in a prison of doubts and insecurities. Sexual abuse significantly contributes to this shame. The Lord, however, can lift our shame. He does not want us to carry it. Resolve to give the shame back. One way to do this is to write a letter to those who shamed you.

To: (perpetrator's name)

I have been carrying the shame of what happened many years ago. I am choosing to stop and to accept the fact that it is not mine. Now I give it back to you. I am going to go on with my life, knowing that in God's eyes I am special. I am unashamed just because I am me—created by Him.

Goodbye, Free and In Christ

This is not a letter to mail. Simply writing it will help break the bondage of shame.

Dear Lord, give me strength to step out of the prison of shame and into the freedom of Your open arms.

> *But we have renounced the hidden things*
> *of shame.*   2 Corinthians 4:2

Psychology is opening many hidden doors of the mind, uncovering reasons for our behavior. Regarding dysfunctional families it is said, "A family is as sick as its secrets."

If we would only look to Scripture, we would find God has already revealed all of this to us. "There is nothing new under the sun." Our secrets become our shame and we are told to renounce the hidden things of shame. We must look at the shame in our lives and disown it, give it up.

Part of our shame has been because of our sexual abuse. By revealing this hidden shame, we can break the power of secrecy and free our children. We must stop the shame now!

Father, help me to acknowledge my hidden shame and release it to You.

The LORD . . . by no means clears the guilty,
visiting the iniquity of the fathers on the children
to the third and fourth generation.

Numbers 14:18

As victims we inevitably ask, "Why did this happen to me?"

One of the reasons we have to consider is generational sin. The Bible is clear about its effects: "Do not be deceived, God is not mocked; for whatever a man sows, that he will also reap" (Gal. 6:7).

A man who practices perversity sows a heritage of perversity for his children, grandchildren, and great-grandchildren. That is why we see incest repeated generation after generation.

This curse can be stopped by repentance. We can be intercessors for our families, praying that the blood of Jesus will cleanse our family bloodlines and break the bondage of generational sin.

Lord, I intercede on behalf of my family. By the power of the blood of Jesus, I pray that the bondage of sexual sin will be broken in my family.

> *Do not remember the inquities of our
> forefathers against us.*
>
> Psalm 79:8 NASV

The generational link to abuse can be devastating. It is not unusual to find incest that has visited a family for generations. One victim yelled, "I can't believe I told my daughter it was her fault. I hated my mother for saying that to me. My daughter must hate me now."

"It's not too late to tell her you'll listen," I replied. I went on to explain that she could be the one to break the chain in her family line. She could be the one who began to break the iniquity. She could pray and repent for the sins of her ancestors and give hope to future generations.

Finally she stood. "I'll be back with my daughter, if she'll talk to me." Her daughter did talk and a reconciliation orchestrated by God took place.

Dear God, please draw our hearts to You. Help us to be the ones who break the link to the sins of our ancestors.

When you pass through the waters, I will be
*   with you;*
And through the rivers, they shall not
*   overflow you.*
                                            Isaiah 43:2

Anyone who has rafted the Colorado River is aware of a place called Separation Canyon. This break in the steep canyon walls beckons one to escape from the treacherous mile-deep gorge that continues.

When Major Powell led the first expedition through there in 1865, three men chose to separate at this point. Fearing for their lives and unable to see an end to the torturous journey filled with raging rapids, they gave up. After separating from the group they were never seen or heard from again. Major Powell and his men pressed on and came to the end of the canyon and its life-threatening rapids less than twenty-four hours later.

How many times do we separate from God when things get really tough and we doubt His promises? Hold fast, for when things look darkest you may be only a breath away from "breaking out of the canyon."

Lord, help me to trust You through the darkest, roughest rivers in my life so that I never separate from You.

> *"For My thoughts are not your thoughts,*
> *Nor are your ways My ways," says the Lord.*
>
> Isaiah 55:8

This was the answer I heard ringing in my ears when I cried out, "No, Lord, this wasn't the way it was supposed to go. I don't think it should happen this way."

Once again my road to recovery was taking an unexpected turn. Actually, I hadn't seen this leg of the journey on any of my maps! The Lord was leaning hard on my control button.

Ah, so that was what was behind all my upset. I was out of control. Things were not going my way. My plans were not being fulfilled. But the Lord was in control. Learning that revealed another issue—trust. Was I willing to trust Him with the course of my recovery? Was I willing to acknowledge that He knows best the path I should take?

Lord, I repent of my need to control. I repent for not really trusting You. Lord, I submit to Your leadership.

*And those who know Your name will put their
   trust in You;
For You, Lord, have not forsaken those who
   seek You.*   Psalm 9:10

As victims of abuse we feel rejected and abandoned and distrustful of others. We often project
these feelings into our relationship with God. We
tell ourselves, "When people we can see prove to be
untrustworthy and forsake us, how can we trust
God, whom we cannot see?"

God is not a man who would forsake or abandon
us. If we don't trust Him, we will go our own way,
making wrong decisions and paying the consequences for them. Ultimately we need to realize
there is no choice but to risk trusting God by taking
a step toward Him. God is faithful to us once we
start seeking Him for answers. When we see His
faithfulness demonstrated it will become easier and
easier to trust Him

*Lord, just today, please give me enough courage to take a step
toward You, trusting that You will not forsake me.*

Indeed, we count them blessed who endure.
James 5:11

Happiness doesn't come from our circumstances. It comes from being at the center of God's will despite our circumstances.

Because of the abusive situations we've endured, many of us focus on environment. We think that if God would just change our circumstances—move us to the country, move us to the city, give us a million dollars, give us a husband, free us from a husband— we would finally be happy. God has never been in the business of changing things; He changes people. His goal for all of us is that we become more like Jesus, whose peace and joy came from knowing He was doing the will of His Father.

When we take our eyes off our circumstances and center ourselves on the Lord, wanting only to be in His will, we will be blessed beyond comprehension in the ways that bring true happiness.

Thank You, Lord, for showing me that true happiness comes from the blessing of being in the center of Your will.

*And not only that, but we also glory in
tribulations, knowing that tribulation produces
perseverance; and perseverance, character;
and character, hope.*　　　Romans 5:3–4

God cares about our circumstances, but He is even
more concerned about our choices. The choices we
make as we persevere during hard times build character.

In order to persevere through an ordeal, we must
choose to believe that God is in control. We must
choose to keep our eyes focused on Him for guidance with our hearts trusting Him. Even in the most
trying and difficult times, we must choose to walk in
peace and joy, accepting His will and timing. Each
one of these choices makes us more like Jesus, and
it is His character in us that will be our victory, guar-
anteeing that we will emerge on the other side.

Let us glorify God for what we must endure and
anticipate His use of our circumstances to produce
in us the character of our Lord.

---

*Thank You, Lord, that through my trials I may develop Your char-
acter, becoming more like You.*

*"Father, I have sinned against heaven and in
your sight, and am no longer worthy to be
called your son." But the father said to his
servants, "Bring out the best robe and put it on
him, and put a ring on his hand and sandals on
his feet. And bring the fatted calf here and kill
it, and let us eat and be merry; for this my son
was dead and is alive again; he was lost and is
found." And they began to be merry.*

Luke 15:21–24

Most of us are familiar with the story of the prodigal son. Receiving his inheritance early in life, he set out on his own. Living unwisely, soon he was living and sleeping in a hog pen.

As sexual abuse victims, have we taken what we thought was our inheritance—a life of shame and brokenness—and allowed it to control our lives? Have we lived unwisely, only to be filled with regrets? Like the prodigal son, we too can repent, receive our Father's forgiveness, and be welcomed back into the family with joy and gladness.

Father, thank You for Your love and for always being ready to forgive us and receive us.

> *And whoever causes one of these little ones who*
> *believe in Me to stumble, it would be better for*
> *him if a millstone were hung around his neck,*
> *and he were thrown into the sea.*
>
> Mark 9:42

Who among us has not experienced rage at being defrauded and robbed of innocence, derailed by the acts of violence against us? Which of us has not thought about revenge?

But "vengeance is mine," the Lord says. Even more specifically, Jesus promises ominous consequences to those who cause children to fall.

We don't need to waste time with thoughts of getting even. God says *He* will repay. When we leave our perpetrators in the hands of God, we also can leave all bitterness and resentment, confident that our all-knowing and just Father is also our advocate and righteous judge. Let's get on with our lives and walk into our futures, free!

Lord, I leave to You the fate of the one who caused me to stumble, and I renounce all thoughts of revenge.

> *He who is without sin among you, let him*
> *throw a stone at her first.* John 8:7

With these words Jesus cut to the heart the band of hypocrites who would have stoned an adulteress. As we read the account, most of us probably accept the story as one of forgiveness and vindication. How would we feel, though, if those same words were addressed to us as we prepared to stone an abuser?

Because of our woundedness, most of us no longer deal with our own sin issues. It is much easier to see the sin against us and to disregard or minimize our own. We are so busy gathering stones to throw that we do not hear the quiet voice of God's Spirit bringing conviction and correction to us.

Forgive me, Lord, for my insensitivity to Your Spirit. I repent of my stone-throwing mentality and invite You now to speak to me about my sin.

He who despises his neighbor sins.
Proverbs 14:21

We don't all respond in the same way to our abuse. Some of us desperately seek a man's attention and approval, while others swear off men forever. Still others vow never to let another man control or dominate them again. For lots of good reasons we despise men. They have used us, abused us, lied to us, made fools of us. . . . And the list goes on and on. They have earned our despisement.

However, the Lord says, whatever our reasons, despisement is a sin. He knows that ultimately there will be consequences for us spiritually, emotionally, and maybe even physically. Despisement is a sin we cannot afford.

We need to repent of our sin and our judgments. We need to release them to the Lord along with all our feelings. Only then can the Lord truly be Lord over the matter.

Lord, I repent of my despisement of men and my judgments against them.

*Bear with each other and forgive whatever
grievances you may have against one another.
Forgive as the Lord forgave you.*

Colossians 3:13 NIV

Lord, how can you expect us to forgive those who have abused us? Oh, the pain. We want them to experience pain and to pay for what they did to us. But this is not God's way. He commands us to forgive as He has forgiven us. How do we do this? Where do we begin?

See your abusers as God sees them, as people He loves. They were probably abused themselves. Victims become the victimizers.

Don't react to your feelings. Instead, seek to see these people as God sees them and love them as He loves them. Miraculously, over time, your anger will lessen. As you look to God, He will fill you with His love and compassion. He will give you the power to forgive sincerely, and in the act of forgiving you will find freedom!

Lord, help me to see my abuser or abusers as you see them. Empower me to forgive them as You have forgiven me.

> *So they went out and preached that people*
> *should repent.*
>
> Mark 6:12

Jesus sent His twelve disciples out with the same message that John the Baptist had preached before Jesus began His ministry. The message was different from the ones the people had always heard. They had always been told to follow all the rules and please men. Now Jesus preached, "Repent for the kingdom of heaven is at hand" (Matt. 4:17).

Repent means to change your heart and mind. Sometimes only God will be able to see this repentance. It may not be flashy or draw attention to itself, but true repentance is an attitude of the heart.

Being a survivor of sexual abuse gave me many bad attitudes from which I needed to repent. Hatred and bitterness had become close friends. I chose to repent, and God changed my heart.

_____

Lord, today I repent of _____. Change my heart.

FINDING LOVE

For a long time
I would not own this part of me;
the hate, the pain,
I'd sealed it in a tomb
and remained its sorry keeper.

Now the door was flung open
and I stayed
and felt the helpless agony
intolerable to a child.

Truth was there
and with it, hope and healing,
in the dung of human tragedy
as Love lay in the stable long ago.

I could not but love her.
Love knew
and gave me room.

> *And Jesus said to them, "I am the bread of life.*
> *He who comes to Me shall never hunger, and he*
> *who believes in Me shall never thirst."*
>
> John 6:35

Piping hot and fresh out of the oven, homemade bread can draw me from miles away! Reading this verse my taste buds and nose are instinctively captivated. But Jesus is not talking about real bread here; He is only using bread as a symbol. He is tenderly telling those around Him that He is the one who will give them spiritual food and keep them alive.

As a child I knew the threat of starvation, both physically and emotionally. Jesus found me hungry, scared, and lonely. He drew me to Him like the aroma of fresh bread draws me. He gave me the nourishment that I needed. He filled me and quenched my thirst. He assures me now that in Him I will never thirst or hunger again.

Because I believe in You, Jesus, I will never hunger or thirst for love again.

But to each one of us grace has been given as
Christ apportioned it. Ephesians 4:7 NIV

I've heard it said that those who have suffered the most loss received the most grace. Survivors of sexual abuse have suffered great losses—the loss of innocence, the loss of purity, the loss of self-esteem, the loss of childhood, and sometimes the loss of memory as we block out the trauma. Those who have not experienced great loss in their lives often marvel at the ability of the abused to survive.

It is truly God's grace, lovingly and abundantly given, that brings us through. He gives us the grace to forgive, the grace to endure the pain (not only of the abuse but of the healing), the grace to love and reach out to others in the same situation, the grace to grow into joy and peace in the Lord.

Wherever we are on the road to healing, let us look to God to give us the grace we need to pursue.

Thank You, Lord, for the grace You have given me in proportion to my loss.

He will feed His flock like a shepherd;
He will gather the lambs with His arm,
And carry them in His bosom,
And gently lead those who are with young.
Isaiah 40:11

My mouth was dry from the desert wasteland, my strength forever drained. Struggling daily to survive, I hungered for a shepherd to feed me and put an end to my wanderings.

Then I met Jesus and lay down at His feet. He gathered me to Him as if I were a lamb without a mother. His strong arms carried me to a safe place where He nurtured me back to health, whispering words of love in my ear. Securely nestled in His warm bosom, I never wanted to leave. But out of the fold He led me, saying, "Go, I will be with you." He now encompasses me. I have no fear, because He is with me.

Jesus heals our bodies ravaged by abuse and revives our spirits crushed by despair. He is our dear Shepherd.

Lead me in Your gentle way, O Lord.

I will not leave you orphans; I will come to you.
John 14:18

What do you see when you think of an orphan? I see a little girl with fear in her eyes. Her dirty little face is streaked with the telltale lines of many tears. Her hair is unkempt and her clothes are soiled and torn. Then I see another girl, an older one. She's been around. She's hard and tough. No one makes her cry.

Maybe this was never you or me, but as victims we felt some of the same feelings. Our abuse left us feeling alone, fearful, tough, and neglected. Although we couldn't trust anyone, we desperately needed someone.

In Jesus Christ, we have that Someone, Someone who has promised He will never leave us orphaned. Someone who will be there whenever we need Him.

Thank You, Jesus, for always being there for me so I never have to be alone again.

> *And the LORD, He is the One who goes before you. He will be with you, He will not leave you nor forsake you; do not fear nor be dismayed.*
> Deuteronomy 31:8

Once again I find myself confused, frustrated, and afraid. I yearn for a companion, a trusted friend who will spend time with me. Someone who is kind and caring, someone full of wisdom and insight to help me find answers to the questions that perplex me.

I believe all survivors of sexual abuse feel this way. Filled with doubts, fear, and distrust, we are isolated and lonely. We crave love and at the same time we spurn love. We desperately need someone to help us sort through our confusion.

When I found Jesus, I found that Someone. He is the answer to all my needs. He fills the void in my heart, for He is the one companion who will never leave me. He goes before me into my darkness and shines His light. I am no longer afraid or dismayed.

Let Jesus be your answer, too.

Thank You, Lord, for You!

He heals the brokenhearted
And binds up their wounds.
Psalm 147:3

Deep inside me, my heart lies broken amid the silent pain. How long shall I know such misery? How long shall I weep? I try to comfort myself as I cradle my hidden secrets alone where no one but God can hear me.

He hears the pain I cannot share and sees the wounds I've worked so hard to hide. If I let Him, He will heal my broken heart and remove my fear and sadness.

Unlike earthly fathers who may abuse and harm us, God the Father wants to repair and restore what Satan has stolen. Let us open our hearts and allow His work to be completed within us. If we are in His love and care, "how long" no longer matters. Content we can rest, knowing that whatever time it takes, He will bring us into healing and wholeness.

Lord, come into my hiding place so that You may heal my heart and bind up all my wounds.

> *Behold, I will do a new thing,*
> *Now it shall spring forth;*
> *Shall you not know it?*
> *I will even make a road in*
> *   the wilderness*
> *And rivers in the desert.*
>   Isaiah 43:19

In 1948 the nation of Israel was re-created in a land laid barren after centuries of abuse and war. Almost all natural wildlife had vanished.

The people took this naked desert and in less than forty years created a land of vast beauty and wealth. Inventing unique methods for irrigation, they produced lush, productive farmlands and covered once-barren areas with trees. Today they are even breeding the wildlife mentioned in the Old Testament to repopulate the area.

Just as these people have brought life to a wasteland, so God can bring life and beauty back to us. Sexual abuse ravages us, leaving us like a wasteland, but God makes us new again, transforming us into beautiful, whole women.

Thank You, Father, for being a God of such power and love that You can take me, naked and wasted, and make me beautiful and whole again.

> *O LORD, You have searched me*
> *and known me . . .*
> *And laid Your hand upon me.*
> Psalm 139:1, 5

Hidden deep within me was a terrified little girl. She was huddled in an empty corner, her small arms wrapped around her chubby, short legs and her tearstained face buried in her tiny lap. She felt totally rejected and utterly abandoned.

In a vulnerable moment I revealed her existence to a trusted friend. She encouraged me to let Jesus enter that secret room. I agreed but immediately felt the little girl's horror and overwhelming shame.

With great compassion, Jesus quietly approached the frightened child. He had always known of her existence and was awaiting this time. He laid His hand on her, gently stroking her hair. His loving touch calmed all her fears. She knew at once that she was safe with Jesus and that He would heal her pain.

Jesus, help me not to be afraid of You. Touch the little girl inside me. Heal her wounds and take away her pain.

> *. . . that you be perfectly joined together.*
> 1 Corinthians 1:10

I believe there was a part of me missing. I felt as though there had been another person within me, a little one distinctly different from who I am today. Her hopes, her dreams, the things she wanted were pushed aside as the years went by. With the blows of life, the little one seemed to die.

Should that part of me be gone forever? Did she really die?

One day while in prayer, I saw Jesus gently holding a little girl. She was me. There was no doubt. But it wasn't me as I am now. It was me as I was then.

I couldn't believe my eyes. The little one I thought had died was in His arms. He called me to join them. He brought us together, and I began to cry, knowing that I would no longer be just a shell of a woman. Jesus had made me complete.

Lord, I thank You that I am perfectly joined together.

*I will give them an undivided heart and put a
new spirit in them.* Ezekiel 11:19 NIV

My tears flowed. My heart was broken and the
adult part of me was grieving. As I recounted the
horror, I cried even harder, for the child part of me
was reliving the abuse. I had always felt like two
pieces of a broken shell—me, the adult, and me, the
child. I was one or the other, and I was never whole.

Now I was weak and exhausted from pouring out
my pain, but all was quiet. Then I felt God's presence as He lifted me in His arms, drew me to His
breast, bound up my wounds, and defused my
memories. Awe filled my soul as I realized that He
was healing the adult and the little girl at the same
time, making me a whole, new person.

A victim of sexual abuse often feels like two people. She can never be whole until the adult and the
child embrace each other and become one. God
promises to do that for us.

Thank You, Lord, for uniting my divided heart, making me one.

> *For You have delivered my soul*
> *from death,*
> *My eyes from tears,*
> *And my feet from falling.*
> Psalm 116:8

You are so emotional."

The accusation deeply wounded me and destroyed the last shred of good I felt about myself. "Lord, why do my emotions cave in so?"

Through healing I've learned that women who experience severe trauma like sexual abuse often get stuck emotionally at the age it occurred. Even though we grow up, we still continue to react to our world and its events through a child's eyes. It is not the adult who needs God's touch, but the little girl within.

Furthermore, we cannot go through emotional healing without being emotional, for only as God leads us through the memories of our past can He bring our emotions into balance.

Father, bring my emotions into line; heal the little girl that's still within. Deliver me from the tears of the past.

*Imitate those who through faith and patience
inherit the promises.*   Hebrews 6:12

It is not uncommon for victims of sexual abuse to feel confused about how to act, how to be a "woman of God." In the past roles were out of order and self-concepts were stained with shame.

One way to find truth and guidance in what God desires for us is to find other women who are solid in the Lord. Learning is imitating. We need to imitate someone who is consistent in her walk with the Lord: studying the Word, living the faith, and practicing the patience God desires in her.

Choose today to find those whom God wants you to imitate and invite them to be in relationship with you. Then study carefully and ask lots of questions. God will bless your desire for renewal with the inheritance of His promises.

Dear Lord, help me to humble myself and reach out to those who can teach me Your ways. Focus my eyes on those You want me to imitate, so that through faith and patience I may inherit Your promise of healing.

> *Loose yourself from the bonds*
> *of your neck,*
> *O captive daughter of Zion!*
> Isaiah 52:2

The Lord has taught me a truth about accountability. I had grown up as a people pleaser, thinking I had to be accountable to everyone in my life who demanded it. I was in bondage as I constantly justified and explained my behavior.

After forty years I finally announced to the Lord, "I am sick of having to explain myself to everybody!" "Good," He responded, "because you only have to be accountable to the few I will show you." What freedom I experienced as I loosened myself from the bondage of "required" accountability and accepted the challenge of healthy accountability.

Think about the people in your life. Those God provides for healthy accountability will speak the truth to you in love, and their lives and wisdom will serve as an example to you.

Loose me, Lord, from the bondage of unhealthy accountability and show me whom to be accountable to.

For your Maker is your husband,
The Lord of hosts is His name.
Isaiah 54:5

Valentine's Day is a day many of us would like to ignore. As victims of sexual abuse, we grew up believing our worth was based upon the attention of men. To be without a boyfriend or with a less-than-intimate husband on Valentine's Day makes us feel like failures who are missing out on the joys of celebrated love.

We don't have to feel that way. The Lord says He is our husband—and not just for single women. He also fills the unmet needs of married women. If we will invite Him into our hearts, He will prove Himself. What better husband could we have than He who created the role?

Let us see what surprises this Valentine's Day brings if we take our eyes off men and put them on Jesus! Let Him be everything and more to us that men have been. We will blossom as He loves us with true and perfect love.

You are my husband, Lord, and I am honored.

> *I am the LORD your God. . . . You shall have no other gods before Me. . . . For I, the LORD your God, am a jealous God.*   Exodus 20:2–3, 5

Everywhere we go, society is trying to sell us the fantasy of romance: to have a mate, a lover, so captivated by you that heaven and earth cannot contain your love for each other.

As abuse victims, we may buy this fantasy and look for a "knight in shining armor" to rescue us. We must realize that this kind of love always leads to disillusionment or love addiction.

God commands us to have no one but Him to fill our hearts and minds. If we make Him our first and truest love, all other relationships come into balance. Loving Him more than any other is the answer to our love hunger.

Father, please help me to guard against anyone or anything else taking first place in my heart.

*And my God shall supply all your need
according to His riches in glory by Christ Jesus.*
Philippians 4:19

As I drove home, my tears began to flow. I had just attended my first support group meeting for sexually abused women. It wasn't what they had shared that caused my pain. It was seeing the concern of a husband who had brought his wife so that she might get help. My thoughts went to my own husband, who didn't seem to know or care where I had gone that evening. I felt so alone.

Things are not always what they seem, however. Weeks later when the group ended, that man had left his wife, while my husband was still with me. I discovered that although my husband was incapable of filling my needs during this time of emotional upheaval, the Lord could richly supply all the love and support I constantly needed.

Let us accept the faithfulness of our spouses and friends during this difficult time, but look to Jesus to fulfill our deeper needs.

Lord, help me press into Your heart when I am needy.

> *Listen to counsel and receive instruction,*
> *That you may be wise in your latter days.*
> Proverbs 19:20

The Lord will do a mighty work of healing through our relationship with Him. In times of prayer and reading His Word, He will touch our wounded hearts. He will give us hope and encouragement and even correction when we need it.

Although there is no substitute for a relationship with Him, He will also use others to help us in our healing process. Godly counselors can be a tremendous support. They can help us understand what we are going through and then guide us through the process.

Aided by counsel and instruction, we will gain the healing and wisdom to overcome our victimization. Then with the Lord's grace we can share with others the pathway to wholeness.

Lord, please bring a source of godly counsel into my life. I thank You now for the wisdom, support, and instruction I will receive.

*But the fruit of the Spirit is love, joy, peace,
patience, kindness, goodness, faithfulness,
gentleness, self-control.*

Galatians 5:22–23 NASV

Because of our pasts, we may have vowed never to
let anyone control us again. As we begin to trust
more in God, we learn to give to the Lord our need
to control. No longer slaves to another's power, we
can finally relax and let God oversee our every moment.

Evidence of our walk with the Lord is the presence of the fruits of the Spirit in our lives. We can
trust His control to produce good results, qualities
we have always wanted.

*Dear Jesus, I trust You and I surrender to You. Bring more of the
fruits of Your Spirit into my life.*

> *For you have had five husbands, and the one*
> *whom you now have is not your husband;*
> *in that you spoke truly.*
>
> John 4:18

Jesus was talking to the woman at the well near Samaria. She was very surprised that a Jewish man would speak to a Samaritan woman, for Jews had no dealings with Samaritans, especially women. Because He is God, Jesus knew all about her relationships with men. He placed no condemnation on her, because He knew that she had been running about from man to man, trying to get filled up. He knows that only He will be able to satisfy her forever.

I was like the Samaritan woman, never having my needs met completely by any man. When I realized my unrealistic expectations I went to the One and only Man, Jesus Christ. He is perfect, the One who can understand all about me and fill my inner being.

Jesus, I have had many "husbands" before you. Forgive me and fill me until I thirst no more.

Present your bodies a living sacrifice, holy,
acceptable to God, which is your reasonable
service.
                                             Romans 12:1

Any man who made a sexual advance toward me
was successful. I abused myself by giving my body
away to anyone who wanted it. I submitted to sex,
all the while craving love that was never there. I was
sacrificing my body to meet an inner need that only
God could fulfill.

Jesus is the only answer to our inner longings. As
we present our bodies to Him, He will fulfill the
deep needs of our hearts, sacrificing Himself for us.
We need but surrender to His will day by day.

Lord, help me to present myself, especially my body, to You today
as a holy instrument for Your service.

> *The heart is deceitful . . . and desperately*
> *wicked; who can know it?*   Jeremiah 17:9

Jesus knows hearts. He knows the hearts of abusers and He knows the hearts of the abused. He knows deceitful hearts and He knows deceived hearts. As abused women, our hearts are deceived, full of false perceptions. We were told lies to justify the abuse, to make us the culprits, to convince us of our unworthiness. All those lies contributed to our misperceptions and affected our whole outlook on life, especially our relationships.

The Lord longs to set us free. The Holy Spirit, superior to the finest computer, knows all our pasts and can reveal truth in our innermost places. Let us be brave and face the lies we have accepted as truth. Let us allow Jesus to correct our misperceptions and to establish new hearts within us.

Lord, You know my heart. Set me free from its deceptions and misperceptions and show me the truth. Help me to have a right perspective on life.

*For this is the will of God . . . that no one
should take advantage of and defraud his
brother in this matter.*

1 Thessalonians 4: 3, 6

The apostle Paul writes to us in this chapter about abstaining from sexual immorality, so that we do not defraud one another sexually. To defraud means to cheat. Many sexually wounded women cheat their husbands of the intimacy that sex can bring. Actually I learned to do just the opposite. My body was out of control and unmanageable. I overcontrolled my emotions, vowing to never give my heart to a man.

Having sex never really bothered me, even though I had been sexually abused for years as a child. That's because I was not there emotionally. For fifteen years of marriage I took advantage of and defrauded my husband. I cheated him of the emotional intimacy of sex. Now, with God's help, I am committed to being there when we have sex.

Lord, I know that only You can see my heart. Help me not to defraud with my body.

> *Let him kiss me with the kisses of his mouth—*
> *For your love is better than wine.*
>
> Song of Solomon 1:2

I went through months of agony trying to come to terms with my sexuality after God had delivered me from past perversions. My "natural" responses seemed dull after a lifetime of sexual behavior based upon impure thoughts and images.

Unable to respond passionately to my husband, I tried to conjure up the methods I had counted on in the past to excite myself as I submitted to sex. But they were gone. I had no more tricks to use.

Sexual abuse not only defrauded me of my innocence in the marriage bed, it deprived me of the opportunity to learn about sex God's way. As I turned to God He restored me. When I confessed my loss, accepted my present situation as temporary, and put our intimacy into His hands, He transformed our lovemaking.

Lord, thank You for bringing me to the place where I can now enjoy the blessings of my sexuality, welcome my husband's kisses, and delight in his love.

For this reason a man shall leave his father and mother and be joined to his wife, and the two shall become one flesh. Mark 10:7–8

Sex is a gift from God to bond husband and wife and make them one. When we have sex with a person outside of marriage, we still become one by the very nature of the sex act, for bonding is the result God intended. Each sexual partner, therefore, leaves his imprint on us.

A major part of our healing will take place when we ask God for the miracle of cleansing. When we allow Him to cleanse us, He removes from our hearts and souls every trace of those men with whom we had sex.

With clean hearts, whiter than snow, we can then enter marriage unhindered, or bring into our marriages a freshness, purity, and oneness we never thought possible.

Thank You, Lord, for cleansing me so that I can now be one with my husband only.

> *Every place that the sole of your foot will tread upon I have given you.*
>
> Joshua 1:3

The Lord still guarantees victory to us, just as He did to Joshua. Like Joshua, it is up to us to take hold of God's promises and bring them to pass.

Take a few minutes to reflect upon your life, to acknowledge the places in your past where you were defiled and robbed. The Lord promises to restore all those painful places. All we have to do is take the responsibility of believing His promise and actively pursue our healing in the places where our feet have trod.

Just think! When we receive Jesus, we become children of the living King who calls us "daughter," "precious," "created for His glory." From Him we receive an inheritance that includes health and wholeness, reconciliation and restoration.

Dear Lord, help me to take possession of the promises You have given me by pursuing my healing in the painful places of my past.

Happy is the man who finds wisdom,
And the man who gains understanding.
Proverbs 3:13

How subtle is the wickedness of Satan! After living more than thirty years in the "humility" of self-contempt and self-hatred, "under the conviction of the Holy Spirit," I realized the truth: This was neither humility nor conviction, but the bondage of condemnation. As long as I held myself in such condemnation, I would be immobile, stuck in sin. God could not act in my behalf until I repented of this attitude.

When I finally understood and confessed my sin, the grace and mercy of God were swift and strong. Within a day I met a new friend, who also had been abused and was not afraid to invest in my healing.

Having survived sexual abuse, let us not fall subject now to Satan's emotional abuse by believing his condemnation. Instead let us seek God's wisdom in our thoughts and attitudes in order to receive His healing.

Lord, thank You for the wisdom and understanding to reject Satan's abuse and receive Your healing.

> *A bruised reed He will not break,*
> *And smoking flax He will not quench.*
>
> Isaiah 42:3

Smoking flax describes the wick of a lamp in which the oil is about gone. It also describes hurting victims of sexual abuse—feeble, weak, barely hanging on.

I felt like that as a young woman. Dad was dead, and I had sworn that I would never allow anyone to hurt and betray me again. I wanted to believe in God, but how could I be sure that God would not damage and destroy me completely? After all, wasn't He called Father? Emotionally bruised and feeble as I was, how could I risk finding out? Yet I sensed that God was the only Way to my healing.

I wept in desperation and confessed my fear and anger, my shame and self-hatred. He neither broke me nor destroyed me. He gently filled me with the faith I lacked. I received Him as my healer and our journey toward wholeness began.

Lord, thank You for Your gentleness when I am weak and feeble.

Do not fear, for you will not be ashamed;
Nor be disgraced, for you will not be put
to shame.
                                        Isaiah 54:4

I couldn't lift my eyes to look at their faces. "What are you afraid of?" my counselor prodded gently.

"I'm afraid to tell my husband what happened to me," I answered, feeling shame grip me. "I'm terrified he will think I'm dirty and never touch me again." He put his arm around me to assure me that was not true.

"It would help him in caring for you if he knew your pain," the counselor encouraged.

My tears seemed never-ending as I revealed the sexual abuse of my past. Unable to look up, I did not know about the tears in my husband's eyes until my counselor told me later.

We carry so much shame over the violations against us that made us feel humiliated and disgraced. Telling the secrets of our pasts in a safe place breaks the shame.

Let us trust Jesus to put the right people in our lives, people with whom we can safely share.

Thank You, Lord, for breaking my shame.

> *Therefore, as God's chosen people . . . clothe*
> *yourselves with compassion, kindness, humility,*
> *gentleness, and patience. . . . And whatever you*
> *do . . . do it all in the name of the Lord Jesus.*
> Colossians 3:12, 17 NIV

My world teetered on the brink. The thought of my brother knowing about the abuse terrified me. But down the hall at that very moment, my counselor was sharing my life story with him. I waited, tormented and still.

Suddenly my brother came around the corner. I fell to my knees and began to cry. He held me in his arms and whispered, "In the name of Jesus, I love you." Never had the love of God felt so real.

The Lord reveals His love to us through His people. His presence in those who truly know Him so magnifies their love that, through them, we feel His powerful touch and experience transformation deep within. Let us look for Him in those who know Him.

Thank You, Jesus, for revealing Yourself to me through the compassion of those who truly love You.

SURPRISED BY GRACE

When I stopped running
and stood still,
when my hands slipped off
my covered eyes
so I could see,
when pain and shame and lies
became great enough
to make me poor,
courage, like a beggar,
challenged me
to call Your name.

Then I saw You,
waiting in my poverty.
You never expected more.

> *Sing to Him a new song;*
> *Play skillfully with a shout of joy.*
>
> Psalm 33:3

In the dark corner of the living room was the old upright piano. The ivory was completely gone from middle C. Other keys were marked and stained and the dark brown frame damaged by small, untrained hands.

Many tunes had been played on her keys to drown out the pain that filled the air. I had resisted the memory of this piano until today, when my own child sat down to play. When everyone was gone, I played a few tunes that lingered in my fingertips. With courage I relived the memories. Tears came to my eyes and I let them flow, no longer holding them back. Soon I noticed the music brought joy. God was making beautiful new songs! For so many years I had hidden that piano, but God wanted to use it. Now each day I sit at His keyboard waiting for His music. I know that whatever tomorrow holds, He will make a new song.

Lord, I am singing a new song today. Thank You.

Praise the Lord O my soul. . . .
I will sing praise to my God as long as I live.
Psalm 146:1–2 NIV

When we are struggling with pain, when we feel empty and alone, our great God gives us the gift of music. No other creatures on earth have the ability to create, duplicate, or thrill to music as humans do! Music can touch our souls when we have reached the bottom and feel nothing but emptiness.

God can touch our spirits with His creative fingers by filling our ears and minds with the beautiful melodies that He has given us. Our God has placed music in our hearts for comfort and healing so that we might be filled with joy and sing praises to His name.

Lord, help me to reach the heavens as I lift my voice in praise to You. May I feel Your presence as You touch my spirit with Your music. Thank You for loving me so much.

> *There is nothing better for a man than that he*
> *should eat and drink, and that his soul*
> *should enjoy good in his labor.*
>
> Ecclesiastes 2:24

A famous comedian once said that she hated housework because you make the beds, do the dishes, and six months later you have to start all over again. Housework, like so many other things in life, has to be done over and over again. There is often no sense of accomplishment with repetitive tasks, yet they still must be done.

Depending on our attitude, we can look upon chores as drudgery or we can put a song in our hearts and do them cheerfully "as unto the Lord."

In working with the memories of our past, our feelings of pain must be dealt with over and over again. If we choose an "attitude of gratitude" we will enjoy the good in our labors and receive healing.

_____

With gratitude, Lord, I offer up the labor of dealing with my past, that I may receive Your healing.

*My soul, wait silently for God alone,
For my expectation is from Him.*
Psalm 62:5

In our home hangs a picture of a young girl leaning against a weather-beaten barn. Her hands clasp a basket of freshly picked field flowers. Her eyes are fixed on the distant lane, watching, waiting.

My life used to be like that, on hold, waiting for some man to take care of me, to meet my needs, to love and accept me.

During the healing process I discovered my real need: Jesus, in His rightful place, on the throne of my heart. In Him I find my identity; from Him spring the love, direction, and satisfaction that I truly need; and through Him all my needs are met.

That passive little figure in the picture is now my constant reminder to wait only on Jesus, eyes fixed confidently on Him.

Thank You, Lord, that I can place my expectations in You, for only You are big enough to fulfill them.

> *You have turned for me my mourning*
>   *into dancing;*
> *You have put off my sackcloth and clothed me*
>   *with gladness.*
>
> Psalm 30:11

Deep inside my protective walls I hold the pain of my life. There seems no peace or hope in store. Tears well up inside me. I long for gentle answers. Are there any for me?

"There are, weary one. Look up!" the Lord says. "I will dry those tears as you lean upon Me. Just trust with all your heart and let restoration begin. A song of joy will spring up and take the place of all those tears."

The Lord, kind and gentle, promises relief, restoration, joy! He requires trust, and trust is what I lack most. But I want His promises more than I fear to trust, so I agree to lean on Him and pray for trust to come.

God wants to transform our weeping and sorrow into dancing and gladness. Let us learn to trust Him and let Him begin the process.

Lord, teach me to trust You, for I desire a song of joy.

> *In the multitude of my anxieties*
> *within me,*
> *Your comforts delight my soul.*
> Psalm 94:19

Physical touch transmits many messages. Sexually damaged women are particularly sensitive to hidden messages that the senders may not realize are being sent. A squeezed arm at the end of a conversation can leave a damaged woman feeling violated. Even worse, she may feel helpless to change the pattern of interaction. Anxiety can become her constant companion as she tries to avoid possible contact.

Jesus gave us the Holy Spirit to comfort us continually with words of encouragement. He promises to be our provider, father, protector, brother, friend. If He is for us, who can be against us? He will support us, and we need no longer allow our anxieties to keep us victimized.

Lord, help me to hear Your words of comfort in all my anxious moments.

What is hidden he brings forth to light.
Job 28:11

It all seemed so real, even the smells were right. Somehow I was back in time and he was standing beside me. Fear gripped my heart and shame covered me like a blanket. Then instantly I was back in the present, my heart racing, my lungs panting, my body trembling. Another flashback had occurred.

At first I fought flashbacks because I did not want the pain. Now I've learned to let them come. Knowing God will heal that which He reveals makes all the difference.

Lord, help me surrender to Your healing process. You will bring to light and heal what is hidden.

My times are in Your hand;
Deliver me from the hand of my enemies,
And from those who persecute me.

Psalm 31:15

Day after day I cried out to my God, "Please, help me! Please make it stop!" Day after day it continued until I could no longer bear the pain. I then made myself enjoy it, but still I felt lonely, lost and cold, hopeless and despairing. I asked myself, "Where is God?"

Then it stopped! God in His grace climbed into my pit, reached out, and took my hand. He pulled me out and in an instant I knew He had always been there. He answered every prayer I prayed; He healed every hurt. He made it stop.

My God, You alone are my helper. Let me never let go of Your hand. You alone are able to deliver me from the hands of my enemies and those who persecute me.

*They shall be safe in their land; and they shall
know that I am the LORD, when I have broken
the bands of their yoke and delivered them from
the hand of those who enslaved them.*

Ezekiel 34:27

Run," was all I heard in my mind, but I could not
move. Everyone around me looked calm while I was
coming apart at the seams. I was trembling, nauseated, and breathing shallow and fast. The racing
feeling inside me produced a throbbing headache.
What had triggered me? Where were these insane
thoughts coming from?

Mental flashbacks are the wounded heart's cry
for healing. My past had come to enslave me again
in the present. However, I cling to the truth that the
Lord always breaks the yoke of enslavement and
brings deliverance. He will not allow the bands of
my perpetrators to enslave me forever.

*Lord, give me the courage to stay in the battle as You break the
yoke of the memories that enslave me. Deliver me, O Lord, from
the bands of those who sinned against me.*

*The thief does not come except to steal, and
to kill, and to destroy. I have come that
they may have life, and that they may
have it more abundantly.*

John 10:10

Sobbing in my bed night after night, I listened for
the footsteps of my abuser coming down the hallway. My mother had recently died and I missed her
desperately. Every night she sat on my bed and
rubbed my growing, aching legs, easing my fearful
heart. Now she was gone. Who would protect me
from the many thieves that would prey upon me?
They stole, they killed, and they destroyed.

Looking for someone to cling to, I turned to the
Creator of life, Jesus Christ. He soothed, rubbed,
and comforted all my aches and pains and He nurtured me. He breathed life into my fearful soul.

Jesus is the only One who can overcome the devastation the thieves worked in our lives. He restores
us and replaces all they destroyed with His abundant life.

Lord, breathe Your life into me.

> *For we do not have a High Priest who cannot
> sympathize with our weaknesses, but was in all
> points tempted as we are, yet without sin. Let us
> therefore come boldly to the throne of grace,
> that we may obtain mercy and find grace to
> help in time of need.* Hebrews 4:15–16

We always had a family dog. Never allowed inside, he lived chained in the backyard, provided with food, water, and occasional attention.

As a child of sexual abuse, I was treated much the same. I was emotionally chained to a father who provided my basic needs and some occasional "attention." I had little more access to him than the family dog.

How wonderful to know that I am a child of God. He cares for me and my needs, and I can go boldly before His throne to receive love, affirmation, and forgiveness.

Thank You, Father, that You are there for me whenever I need You.

*The Spirit of the Lord is upon Me, because He
has anointed Me to preach the gospel to the
poor. He has sent Me to heal the brokenhearted,
to preach deliverance to the captives.*

Luke 4:18

As a child I walked each day with my head hung
low, fearing someone might know my dark secret.
How I hated the nights to come. I feared he would
be there, hiding in the hallway or behind a door. I
wished I had told my brother; he might have kept
me safe. But I was just ten and didn't know what to
do.

A year ago I was introduced to our Lord Jesus. He
set me, the captive, free from the fear of the past.
He even healed my scars and gave me freedom
from all the dark secrets that were locked away. I
know He wants to bring complete wholeness to all
those who come to Him. This is liberty only He can
offer.

*Jesus, help us to come to You, that we might be healed and set
free.*

> *For you shall go out with joy,*
> *And be led out with peace.*
> Isaiah 55:12

I think about each room as I walk again down the hallway of my memory. Behind each door there was either physical or emotional pain. As I walk slowly I remember the abuse as a small child, the hiding from a stepfather as a young girl, and the sorrow of being an adult. The sting of pain was in every room, but the darkness and fear are gone now.

My friend Jesus has made the difference. Day by day I entered a different room with Him. As I relived each experience, Jesus healed and restored me, filling each room with light. I've come out of the rooms of the past with joy and peace.

Thank you, Lord, for releasing me from the horrors of the past and for leading me in joy and peace.

He leads me beside the
still waters.
He restores my soul.
Psalm 23:2–3

This psalm depicts the journey of the Good Shepherd and His sheep. The Good Shepherd leads the flock, going ahead to ensure their safety and to make provisions for them.

While there may be obstacles and difficulties on the journey, there will also be times of rest and refreshment. The Shepherd searches out places where there are still waters, waters of rest. In those places the sheep can relax and drink fresh, pure water.

As sheep of His pasture we too need places of quiet refreshment. We need to follow His lead and drink the Living Water of His Spirit. In such places of rest our hearts and minds will be restored by the Shepherd of our souls.

Lord Jesus, help me follow You to still waters. I desire, Lord, to find rest and restoration for my soul in You.

*Are you the Coming One, or do we look
for another?*

Matthew 11:3

How do I reclaim my life? My father was my enemy, and he is dead! Am I to smile and say, "It's okay! He's dead now. I forgive him"? How do I forgive when there is no strength of love in my heart?

I was searching for answers. Was I even searching in the right places? I cried, "Lord, are you the right one, or should I look for another?"

Then came the soft promptings of His Spirit, "The enemy is sin. Look within. Acknowledge the pain, anger, fear, and shame. Look at them eye to eye. I am with you always. I have grace for you. I will be your strength and your healing."

The Lord Jesus is the One we must look to in our soul-searching pain. Only He has the right answers.

*Thank You, Lord, that I don't have to look further. You are my
answer.*

> *Out of the same mouth proceed blessing and*
> *cursing. . . . Does a spring send forth fresh*
> *water and bitter from the same opening?*
> James 3:10–11

These words shook me. I was at my first Bible study, and the Lord was wasting no time. He quickly showed me that my tongue was out of control.

Most of the time I was warm and loving. However, I was also prone to occasional nasty outbursts when I was angry. In such a state I attacked anyone in my path.

I quickly repented and asked the Lord to change me. Little did I know that the answer to my prayers would bring a deep healing to me.

The Lord let me see that my verbal outbursts were my unconscious way of retaliating for my abuse. I had been victimized sexually. Those unhealed wounds fed my angry words. I was unknowingly victimizing others and allowing the cycle of victimization to continue.

Thank You, Lord, for healing my wounds and putting an end to the cycle of victimization.

> *"Be angry, and do not sin": do not let the sun*
> *go down on your wrath.* Ephesians 4:26

Must anger generate violence? When I get angry, I want to hurt someone or break something! Since it's not Christ-like to behave this way, I turn that anger inward instead. I hurt myself by doing things that aren't good for me. I eat too much, eat the wrong kinds of food, or go on a shopping spree that I can't afford.

Most of our wrong behavior is a carryover from childhood. Because we were unable to safely express our pain, fear, and anger at the sexual abuse, we learned to stuff those emotions and vent them indirectly against others or against ourselves.

Emotions turned inward are just as destructive as emotions turned outward. As Creator of emotions, God knows the appropriate way to express them in order to achieve the purpose for which they were created.

Let us ask Him to break our wrong patterns of reacting and to teach us right responses.

Father, teach me Your way of responding to emotional situations.

> *Let all bitterness, wrath, anger, clamor and evil*
> *speaking be put away from you, with all malice.*
> Ephesians 4:31

As injured and scarred women we could easily become bitter and stay that way. Many of you may be bitter now, full of anger and unforgiveness toward the person or persons responsible for your abuse.

But our heavenly Father does not want the poison of bitterness to permeate our lives. He wants to cut it out and fill the empty space with His love. Our Lord is a God of great compassion and unconditional love. His example to us of this love was shown through His Son, Jesus Christ.

Let go of the bitterness. Give it to the Lord. If you hang onto it, it will only eat away at your innermost being until you are consumed. You will become a sick, ugly, hard person. Instead forgive and receive the full benefit of our Lord's love.

Heavenly Father, help me to let go of the anger and bitterness. Help me to forgive my abusers as You have forgiven me.

> *When my father and my mother forsake me,*
> *Then the LORD will take care of me.*
>
> Psalm 27:10

It was hard for me to accept that my parents had forsaken me. As a child, I blamed only the perpetrator for the abuse.

Gradually I began to see that my parents had failed to fulfill their God-given role in my life. My father was emotionally absent. My mother, although awakened nightly by my screams, never heard me with her heart. They failed to protect me, and when I desperately needed their intervention I was forsaken.

The Lord, however, did not forsake me. He took care of me. He engineered circumstances that removed me from the abuse. He made a way of escape for me.

_____

When my father and my mother had forsaken me, You took care of me, Lord. Thank You for Your tender loving care!

> *In the multitude of my anxieties*
> *within me,*
> *Your comforts delight my soul.*
> Psalm 94:19

As we become more healthy and whole, God will begin to speak to us about taking additional steps toward fulfilling His plans for us. He will ask us to do some things that will take us out of those warm, cozy spots we settled into as we received our healing. He will nudge us out of our nests to try our wings, for we cannot mature by clinging to the nest, nor can we grow by sitting still.

This may cause us to feel a multitude of anxieties! But the promise of His Presence beside us and of His Spirit guiding us gives us the confidence to step out in obedience, trusting the results to Him. We must try our wings, for only then can we soar!

I delight in Your comfort, Lord, when my heart is anxious. Thank You for giving me the confidence to fly!

> *But God is faithful, who will not allow you to be*
> *tempted beyond what you are able, but with the*
> *temptation will also make the way of escape,*
> *that you may be able to bear it.*
>
> 1 Corinthians 10:13

Escaping from reality has become a national pastime. The need to escape is powerful. People want to medicate life's pain away. They may use drugs, alcohol, food, sex, or power to try to control their environment. But soon they find the "medication" has control of them, and they are victimized by a new tormentor.

As abused women, we're often tempted to take matters into our own hands. But Jesus wants us to escape our sin, not reality. When we allow Him to be in control of our lives, we will no longer give in to the temptation to medicate. He offers us a healthy choice that heals the wounds and removes the pain.

Lord, help me to make You my means of escape.

Wait on the LORD;
Be of good courage,
And He shall strengthen your heart;
Wait, I say, on the LORD!

Psalm 27:14

In today's world of instant everything we become impatient with ourselves, our relationships, our difficulties, and our pain. We want instant cure for our abuse. God tells us to wait. He works in His way and in His time. As we learn to wait on Him, we can expect to find hidden treasures. We learn patience, receive His peace, discover His joy, and develop courage.

During the difficult times wait patiently on God. Allow Him to speak to your heart and heal your wounds. He knows your every need and what it will take to heal you.

Give Him control of your life and wait on Him.

Lord, give me the courage and patience to wait on You to work in my life.

> *Do not be wise in your own eyes; fear the Lord
> and shun evil. This will bring health to your
> body and nourishment to your bones.*
>
> Proverbs 3:7–8 NIV

I have found that one of the strongholds I battle is control. Because I was abused, I did not want to be helpless again. As the years passed, I became a leader in church groups, making it easier to mask the control in the guise of serving others. Fortunately the Lord brought people into my life who graciously pointed out my shortcomings. I had become wise in my own eyes, depending only on myself.

Lord, I repent of being wise in my own eyes. Help me release control to You, trusting it will bring health to me.

> *For to be carnally minded is death, but to be*
> *spiritually minded is life and peace.*
>
> Romans 8:6

I'd like to go to the roping Sunday," my husband said. An argument ensued. If I let him go this Sunday, he would surely spend every Sunday at the roping arena.

The Lord whispered in my heart, "Let him go; release him." "Could that be You, Lord?" I asked. It was, and I spent the following morning with Jesus, tearfully releasing the control I had exercised for years.

It wasn't easy, for control was my biggest issue. Like most victims of sexual abuse, I had reacted with a vow never to be controlled again. When I became a Christian, I added a qualifier to that vow—"except by the Lord." Now I saw that needing to control my husband meant I had never fully surrendered to Jesus.

When I surrendered, the results were astounding! My husband and I began to enjoy each other and our time together. And the roping arena never did become his Sunday pastime.

Our carnal minds want control, but surrender brings life.

Lord, I surrender my mind to the control of Your Spirit.

> *Perseverance must finish its work so that you*
> *may be mature and complete, not lacking*
> *anything.*
>   James 1:4 NIV

Healing brings recognition. We see things we never saw before.

One day, I "saw" the many arrogant men in my life. It seemed as if every male who was important to me was all-knowing, all-seeing, and all-controlling. As I looked back over my life with newly opened eyes, I saw it had always been that way.

Recognition brought discontent. I wanted to run and leave behind all those men who still treated me as the victim I once was; however, it wasn't to be that easy. God's desire was for me to stay and learn how to deal with those arrogant men.

He required me to persevere, not escape. As I did I matured, and the men in my life responded to the changes in me. Obedience to God's will isn't always easy, but we experience the joy of restoration when we do things His way.

Thank You, Lord, for giving me the strength to persevere.

> *Let the LORD be magnified,*
> *Who has pleasure in the prosperity*
> *of His servant.*   Psalm 35:27

Depending on which end of a spyglass you look through, it magnifies and draws the object closer or it minimizes and sets the object at a distance.

When we observe the wounds in our lives they often become magnified and tower over us, while our God becomes small and distant. It is the work of the Holy Spirit in our lives that reverses the spyglass and reveals our circumstances as they truly are. Our God is magnified and our troubles are diminished. As we observe Him as He is, the wounds of life are healed and we will prosper.

Be magnified in my life, O Lord.

> *He is despised and rejected by men,*
> *A man of sorrows and acquainted with grief. . . .*
> *But He was wounded for our transgressions,*
> *He was bruised for our iniquities.*   Isaiah 53:3, 5

When we look upon Jesus we need to remember that He was despised, rejected, and wounded. He experienced sorrow and grief.

When we look at ourselves and those around us, we need to remember that all of us have been wounded. Some of us have been despised or rejected. Nearly all of us are acquainted with sorrow and grief. Because of our woundedness we all have committed transgressions.

Our wounds give rise to sin and more wounding. Jesus' wounds give rise to forgiveness and healing. He alone can both understand and bring an end to our sorrow and grief.

Thank You, Jesus, for suffering so I can be free from sin and healed of my wounds.

For the LORD does not see as man sees; for
man looks at the outward appearance, but
the LORD looks at the heart. 1 Samuel 16:7

Sometimes the pain of feeling unloved and rejected seems more than I can bear. It feels like no one really loves me for who I am, only for what I can do for them.

This is because many people tend to look only at the surface behaviors. It's also because people—especially abusers—can be selfish, self-centered, and too much into their own pain to see beyond their needs to the heart of another.

We cannot be like that. We must look beyond our needs and see that people have hurts, needs, and desires.

Father, give me the ability to ignore the outward appearance of those I meet and see into their hearts.

> *I will give you a new heart and put a new spirit*
> *within you; I will take the heart of stone out of*
> *your flesh and give you a heart of flesh.*
>
> Ezekiel 36:26

Often as abuse victims we have learned to harden our hearts. We have done this as a protection against the emotional pain of the past. Unfortunately a hardened heart not only feels less pain, it also feels less love. We may lack compassion and sensitivity toward others.

We must be willing to allow God to replace our hearts of stone. By trusting Him to bear our pain, He will give us hearts of flesh, tender enough to receive love while being sensitive to the needs of others.

Father, I offer to You my heart of stone. Replace it with a heart of flesh.

It is good to give thanks to the LORD,
And to sing praises to Your name,
O Most High.   Psalm 92:1

The word *victim* implies that a person is still living a life of abuse. Some of us find it difficult to overcome our victimization and the memories of our past.

I found that one way to go forward was to have a "praise feast." Every day for thirty days, I looked for everything I could thank God for. On the days I felt the most depressed, I thanked Him for flowers or mountains or a warm shower. It was amazing that each day I found more to praise God for, and the negative thoughts began to fade away.

When I find myself slipping back to the abuse, I do another praise feast.

Today, Father, help me to see what I can give thanks for and renew my heart so I can sing praises to Your name, O Most High!

> *Look unto Jesus, the author and finisher of our faith, who for the joy that was set before Him, endured the cross.*
> Hebrews 12:2

Jesus endured the pain of the cross because He knew what His suffering and death would accomplish.

Many times I need to be reminded of the joys in store for me if I can endure the pain of my cross. Unless I am willing to face the memories and endure their pain, I can never know true joy.

We have the assurance that God is with us every step of the way. We need to fix our minds on the final outcome in order to endure the present pain. He will finish what we cannot do.

Lord Jesus, help me to focus on the joy I will know when I am healed.

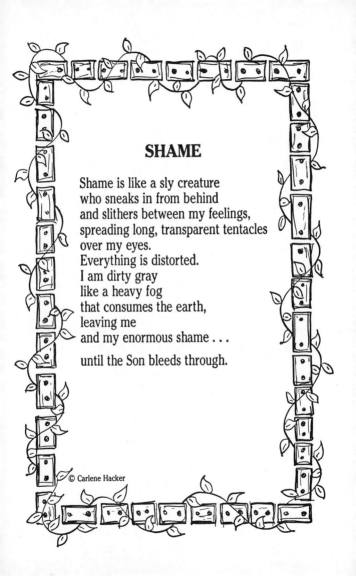

SHAME

Shame is like a sly creature
who sneaks in from behind
and slithers between my feelings,
spreading long, transparent tentacles
over my eyes.
Everything is distorted.
I am dirty gray
like a heavy fog
that consumes the earth,
leaving me
and my enormous shame . . .

until the Son bleeds through.

> *Instead, speaking the truth in love, we will in*
> *all things grow up into him who is the Head,*
> *that is Christ.*
>   Ephesians 4:15 NIV

Consider the key thoughts in today's quotation: truth . . . love . . . grow up . . . Head . . . Christ. We can see them as building blocks. The foundation is truth. If we believe the truth of who we are in Christ, shame will not shatter our lives. If the commitment to love is placed upon the truth, it gives us the ability to minister to others' needs and not be so focused on our own. Upon that love, we can grow the way the Lord has planned for us, for He makes our footing stable. And at the top, the head, we place Christ. In that way our direction is guided by His viewpoint, not ours. We can't put these blocks in order by ourselves. We need guidance from others and the help of God the Master Builder, to cement them in place with the mortar of His ways and His word.

Dear God, build me, help me grow up in You.

> *The steps of a good man are ordered*
> *by the Lord.*　　Psalm 37:23

Aha! At last I knew God's will. I knew what my future held, and I was prepared to accept it. In my mind I planned accordingly, working through the feelings and envisioning what it would be like. Then suddenly the ground shifted, and I no longer knew which way I was headed. I had been so sure of God's instruction; I was sure I'd heard Him right.

We often think we know what God is doing, but He rarely gives us the whole picture all at once. Just as He has ordered our healing one step at a time, so He orders our lives. Instead of taking the instruction for just one step and jumping to conclusions, let us trust God to lead us to the goal He has in mind.

Thank You, Lord, for ordering my steps. Help me not to jump to conclusions about Your goal for me but to be content with one step at a time.

*Grace, mercy, and peace from God our Father
and Jesus Christ our Lord.*   1 Timothy 1:2

We who have been shamed and deeply wounded desperately need the grace, mercy, and peace of God. It is by grace that we walk the road to recovery. His all-sufficient grace empowers us, making us more than conquerors. Because His mercies are new every morning, He leads us to the place of healing. There, by the abundance of His mercy, we find rest and relief even from our own sins.

In resting we experience His peace, which passes all our understanding. His peace alone settles all our internal storms.

By the grace, mercy, and peace of the Father and Christ Jesus, we endure the pain and gain a lifetime of wholeness in Him.

Thank You, for Your never-ending grace, mercy, and peace.

*It shall come to pass
That before they call, I will answer;
And while they are still speaking, I will hear.*
                                        Isaiah 65:24

My legacy was one of not being heard. In my family children were not viewed as real people with anything important to say. So, as a child trapped in a nightmare of incest, I tried to communicate my plight, but no one heard.

The horror of abuse followed me into marriage. How could I have known I would marry an abuser? I cried out for help, but again no one heard. No one understood. Now I know there was One who heard. There was One who understood my private hell. If only I had known God then, how different it might have been.

But what a comfort now to know that He will answer when I call. What a comfort to know that He hears me when I speak. What a blessing to know I am no longer alone.

Thank You, Lord, for hearing and answering me.

> *For You have formed my inward parts . . .*
> *I will praise You, for I am fearfully and*
> *wonderfully made.*   Psalm 139:13–14

Even though I was a girl, they wanted a boy. I didn't want to disappoint them, so I played the role well. Everyone seemed to be pleased.

Women who have been sexually damaged try to find favor in this way and often reject their feminine bodies.

God formed us as we are. He wants us to accept our bodies as a gift to be appreciated and enjoyed. He wanted a little girl even if my parents wanted a boy.

Jesus, help me to see my body as fearfully and wonderfully made, not as a mistake.

*Do not let your beauty be that outward
adorning . . . but let it be . . . a gentle and quiet
spirit, which is very precious in the sight of God.*
1 Peter 3:3–4

I spent my life ashamed of my looks, always comparing myself to other women. I felt inferior; the shame ran deep. I was afraid to let go and be silly for fear I would look foolish; I never participated in sports because I ran "funny." Everything I did and didn't do had to do with how I looked.

I never fully lived until I came to know the Lord. I found He wasn't interested in my outward looks; He valued what was inside me. He was interested in my heart.

Let us give our shame to the Lord and yield to His love. As we dwell in His presence, we need not worry about our outward appearances.

Dear Lord, develop a gentle and quiet spirit within me.

> *To You, O Lord, I lift up my soul. . . .*
> *Turn Yourself to me, and have mercy on me,*
> *For I am desolate and afflicted.*
>
> Psalm 25:1, 16

It's 3:30 P.M., and the last bell of the day has rung. As I leave the building to catch the school bus, a sadness creeps over me. By the time the bus gets to my stop, all the laughter and happiness of the day are completely gone. At home I enter a world of secrets, fear, shame, and hiding. I hate being a girl.

Years have come and gone since those school days, but the pain and sorrow remained. Not until Jesus came into my life could I lift up my head and receive the healing He had prepared for me.

As survivors of sexual abuse, we don't like ourselves and we don't trust others. But if we can summon enough trust to lift our souls to Jesus, He will release us from the oppression of heartache, loneliness, and affliction. He will bring us into peace with our pasts and into acceptance of ourselves.

Thank You, Lord, that when I turned to You, You heard my prayer.

Above all, taking the shield of faith with which you will be able to quench all the fiery darts of the wicked one. Ephesians 6:16

Before heading into battle, we are told to take the shield of faith. A man-made shield will become worn in battle, but the shield of faith God has given us becomes stronger as it is used to stop the fiery arrows of doubt from our enemies.

Our loving Father guards and protects us, knowing the strength of our shield of faith. Every time we risk using it we trust Him to be there, guiding us, never leaving our sides. Each time we use the shield, our faith in God is strengthened.

The Lord wants to accomplish something in us or through us with each battle, so we need only hold up the shield of faith and step forward in confidence.

Lord, thank You for the battles in life by which my faith in You is strengthened. May I never doubt You.

> *You have given me the heritage of those who
> fear Your name.*
>
> Psalm 61:5

You can hold a grudge better than anyone I've ever met," my husband remarked.

"I learned from experts," I replied. "My grandmothers were masters at it!"

Although my reply was glib, I realized I came from a line of bitter, angry, victimized women. Each generation poisoned the next with their bitterness and angry talk. It became clear that my grudges were more than just my sin. I had a heritage that helped give rise to them.

However, I have access to a new heritage in Jesus Christ. By repenting and giving my heritage to Him, the power of my family sin was broken. Then I was free to embrace the heritage of those who fear His name.

Lord, thank You for giving me a new heritage in You.

*Do not be terrified, or afraid of them. The LORD
your God, who goes before you, He will fight
for you.*   Deuteronomy 1:29–30

Fear is a terrifying thing! A destructive force! It starts with a knot in the pit of the stomach and swiftly moves throughout the body. Once it has a hold on me, I am incapable of thinking clearly or acting. I become frozen, my pulse races, and I feel out of control.

Our heavenly Father says over and over in Scripture, "Do not be afraid. Do not be terrified. I go before you and I will fight for you."

Now when I feel the knot of fear begin to rise in me, I call upon my God and remind myself I have no need to fear. The Lord goes before me and fights for me!

Father, help me to hang on to Your words of assurance and know that You fight for me. I have no need to fear.

> *I sought the Lord, and He heard me,*
> *And delivered me from all my fears.*
>
> Psalm 34:4

One of my greatest fears was that if people really knew what I was thinking they wouldn't like me. So I stuffed my thoughts and feelings, which only forced them to come out in other destructive ways. My children suffered because of my displaced anger. I was a pendulum that would swing from being controlling and possessive on the one hand to being passive and a doormat on the other, depending upon the person I was with.

Giving in to our fears by stuffing our feelings is deceitful to our family and friends, but we are the ones who suffer most. For me, the years of stuffing that began with the sexual abuse resulted in chronic physical pain.

God wants to set us free from our fears and their destructions and teach us new and healthy ways of living. Let us seek the Lord and receive His deliverance.

Thank You, Lord, for delivering me from fear and for teaching me to walk in health.

And thus the secrets of his heart are revealed.
1 Corinthians 14:25

I attended yet another healing seminar. Maybe this time God would heal me from the emotional and physical pain I had experienced for almost twenty years. When the pastor announced the Lord's desire to heal headaches, I went forward. "Did something happen just before the headaches started?" he asked. My heart sank. I was in front of the congregation with no place to hide. My shame grew as I realized they would all know about me. Fortunately my desire for healing was stronger than my shame, and I knew I had to do whatever it took. I revealed my secret—I had been raped at the age of eighteen.

God not only healed me of my headaches that evening, He also opened a door of freedom. Other women who had been victims of rape also revealed their heartbreaking secrets.

Help me, Lord, to become willing to reveal the hidden secrets of my heart in order to receive Your healing.

The entrance of Your words gives light.
Psalm 119:130

Do you remember as a child how everything was more scary in the dark? Shadowy objects looked bigger than life. Noises seemed much louder in the still dark of night. Ordinary sounds somehow were eerily transformed and became unrecognizable.

My journey to recovery has taught me the same lessons. Those things that I so carefully kept in the dark recesses of my mind had grown to unmanageable proportions. The memories, guilt, and shame became overwhelming. My life was a nightmare—day and night.

It was not until I sought counsel that things changed. The changes came because my inner fears and pain were brought into the light. Someone dispelled my darkness by speaking words of love and acceptance. I was assured that God was not mad at me and that He didn't blame me for what was done. His words brought light to my darkness and healing to my soul.

Thank You, Lord, that the light of Your words dispels the darkness.

> *He also brought me up out of*
> *a horrible pit,*
> *Out of the miry clay,*
> *And set my feet upon a rock,*
> *And established my steps.*
> Psalm 40:2

Throughout my childhood and teenage years, I felt as though I had done something terribly wrong. Later incidents reinforced my negative thoughts about myself. Like the time my employer fondled me and rather than confront him, I quit.

Quitting didn't totally solve my problem. I continued to be violated by men, and often asked, "Why me?"

Self-pity became my new friend, and as I nurtured it, my growth stopped. I resorted to pat answers of "You just don't understand" or "I can't do that." I was stuck in the miry clay.

In spite of my self-pity God was faithful. He showed me I had two choices: stay in the pit or venture out by His grace. When I chose to risk, He set my feet on firm ground and got me growing again.

Lord, help me out of the horrible pit of my self-pity. Thank You for being the Rock upon which I can set my feet. Establish my steps.

> *But if we walk in the light as He is in the light,*
> *we have fellowship with one another.*
>
> 1 John 1:7

The morning began with the sounds of my father beating my mom in the next room. Later that morning he took my friend and me for a ride. After molesting both of us, he took us to see my sister who was in the hospital. Dad told me it was my fault she was there because she and I had been fighting.

I remember thinking that anyone I cared about would be hurt, and it would be my fault. I vowed not to be close to anyone because I was so bad. Unfortunately that vow created great loneliness within me.

As I shared this memory with my counselor, I began to sob uncontrollably. As we prayed, I knew Jesus wanted to take away my loneliness. The counselor explained that such vows are often made in the midst of torment, based on our feelings, not on God's truths. I chose to renounce that vow, and now my loneliness is gone.

Lord, show me the light of Your truth, especially the wrong inner vows I've made that keep me from fellowship with others.

Watch with Me.
Matthew 26:40

Why did God allow this abuse?

Doesn't He love me?

Why must I suffer this pain?

As I faced the Lord with these questions, I grew closer to Him. The intimacy became more important than the answers.

I now know that He doesn't just want us to focus on our pain and problems. He wants us to be with Him, to watch with Him, to share our hearts and hear His.

Lord, help me not only to share my heart but to listen to Yours.

> *For this is the will of God, your sanctification:*
> *that you should abstain from sexual immorality.*
> 1 Thessalonians 4:3

My inability to resist sexual advances was fixed by the age of twelve. The incredible risks I took to be "loved" during the ten years that followed indicate how far removed I was from reality. I gave barely a thought to possible consequences, the severe punishment, and public humiliation that would have ensued if I had been found out.

Yet even as I threw caution to the wind, I was very much aware of my sin and deepening shame. Marriage would surely erase that and make me feel "right" again. Ironically, I found sex in marriage boring. Sex without risk held no allure. At thirty-eight years old, defrauded, perverted, and tainted, I turned to Jesus.

Sexual abuse perverts our sexuality and taints our intimacy. But Jesus can cleanse us and restore our purity to a point some of us have never experienced.

Thank You, Lord, that as we renounce our immorality, You sanctify us, set us apart, and use us for Your glory.

*For offenses must come, but woe to that man
by whom the offense comes!*   Matthew 18:7

I couldn't believe that if there is a God, He would allow this to happen to me, an eight-year-old child. I knew very little about God, but I believed He was good. Denying the abuse and the abuser was my attempt to protect my hope that God exists.

"Lord, why didn't you help me?" is the legitimate cry of every broken heart. We are compelled to ask the question, but we need to realize that belonging to Him does not take away the reality of sin and its effect in our lives. Then we can be free to acknowledge the damage to our souls without shame or fear of denying the truth of the Gospel. When we can believe God is trustworthy, the lies and denial are no longer necessary. We can face the offense, receive our healing, and leave the offender to God.

Lord, thank You for helping me face the reality of the offenses without denying You.

> *For You, LORD, have made me glad*
>   *through Your work;*
> *I will triumph in the works of*
>   *Your hands. . . .*
> *A senseless man does not know,*
> *Nor does a fool understand this.*
>
> Psalm 92:4, 6

Thank You, Lord, for my sexual abuse. "Absurd!" you say. But wait—listen to what the psalmist says. "You, Lord, have made me glad through Your work." God can take the abuse we have suffered, heal our wounds, and use us to show His powerful works to the unbelieving world around us.

Through God we can triumph over our pain. The godless of this world will not understand how we can find gladness in such circumstances, but we can demonstrate the love and grace of our heavenly Father, through victory, in our lives. Praise the Lord!

Thank You, Father, for the pain of abuse I have suffered, for You are able to turn it into gladness and triumph.

Blow the trumpet in Zion,
And sound an alarm in My holy mountain!
Let all the inhabitants of the land tremble;
For the day of the LORD is coming,
For it is at hand.

Joel 2:1

Trumpets were blown loudly in Bible days. They called people to prayer, to worship, or to war. Some trumpets were made of metal and some were made of a ram's horn. Hearing the horn meant to be on the alert, watch out, and prepare. This verse warns of God's coming judgment.

The judgment day of the Lord comes for all of us. God will rightly judge us and those who have abused us. But we need not endure God's judgment if we turn to Him and plead for mercy. God sent His mercy through His Son, Jesus Christ. It is God who has shown us mercy for our sins. We can leave the land that we inhabited, and we will not tremble when we hear the horn blow.

Blow the trumpet soon, Lord, and may my abusers turn to You, pleading for mercy.

Are the consolations of God too small for you?
Job 15:11

When abuse fills us with pain, often our response is to hide the hurt and pretend it didn't happen. We should not continue to hide our pain; we need to openly share what was hidden for so long.

However, sometimes we go too far in telling other people about the wound, the shame, the unfairness of it all. We want to get sympathy. We want to be affirmed. We want everyone to be on our side! Certainly a wise confidant is a blessing from God, but amassing an army of supporters can only enlarge the problem—it won't resolve our pain.

God's consolations always go right to the heart of the issue, perfectly addressing our deepest needs. We will find his consolations in quietness, in His Word, and in wise counsel.

Lord, teach me to value Your consolation, Your wisdom, Your tender touch in my life more than the sympathy of others.

My beloved is mine, and I am his.
Song of Solomon 2:16

As I began to be healed, I became acutely aware of my lack of emotion during sexual intimacy with my husband. My emotional detachment allowed me to watch myself as I mechanically went through the motions and to hear myself as my self-talk reflected this detachment. It was as if I were on the outside watching, giving commentary on each move—commentary filled with resentment, punishment, and a struggle for control.

My new awareness also helped me recognize that I had relegated my husband to the role of scapegoat, an innocent man suffering for the guilty men in my past. This revelation was a turning point in my healing. I began to separate my past from my present, my husband from the abusers, his love from their lust.

The Lord delivered me from giving double messages of love/hate, messages of confusion that hurt my husband. I was able to truly become his lover.

Lord, give me the freedom to fully be my husband's lover.

> *Then God saw everything that He had made,*
> *and indeed it was very good.* Genesis 1:31

Upon learning that dissociating and "performing" sexually are not characteristics of healthy intimacy, I wrote myself a letter. I gave myself permission to enjoy sex with my husband, to welcome it, desire it, and even to initiate it.

I explained to myself that God created sex between a husband and wife to be a blessing, an act of oneness and joy. I reminded myself how I had first learned about sex and then declared myself free of the things I was taught and the way I was taught them. I acknowledged the power of Jesus to cleanse and heal. Finally, I encouraged myself to renew my mind with His word and to remember that He says, "It is good."

Thank You, Lord, for the blessing of sex as You created it. Help me to see it as good!

Who can find a virtuous wife?
For her worth is far above rubies.
Proverbs 31:10

Your marriage may not make it," the speaker warned. Fear gripped my heart. Of all the anxieties I experienced as I weighed the cost of getting well, the fear of losing my marriage was the most devastating.

I experienced many changes as I was set free from my past, for I became more like God meant me to be. As I changed, the dynamics of my marriage and other relationships changed. My emotional health threatened my husband as he adjusted to these changes.

Becoming a virtuous woman means becoming a force for good. Much to my surprise and pleasure, my changes brought healthier, more fulfilling behaviors to our marriage. I found myself encouraging my husband when I used to be the one always needing support. My honesty provoked his; my willingness to deal with problems changed his responses as well. It was difficult, but we both grew as I became more virtuous.

Seeking the Lord and His plan for our lives means we must be willing to surrender everything to Him, including our marriages, trusting Him for the outcome.

Lord, I want to become a virtuous woman and I trust the results to You.

> *Now acquaint yourself with Him and*
> *be at peace.*
>
> Job 22:21

When are you going back to work?" they asked.
After years of working outside the home, I had been
laid off. "Never, I wish! I love being home."

"But what do you do all day?"

How could I express to my friends the contentment I'd found spending my days with the Lord?
God's perfect timing allowed me to focus on the
things He was uncovering as we walked through
my healing. When that special time ended and He
provided a job, I grieved my loss of unhurried time
with Jesus, who had become my best friend.

God will arrange for each of us to spend time
alone with Him if we let Him. He'll teach us, heal us,
and bestow His peace and joy while granting the
most awesome blessing of all—the gift of knowing
Him.

———

Thank You, Lord, that You created me to know You, walk with
You, and talk with You. I am at peace in Your marvelous pres-
ence.

How sweet are Your words to my taste,
Sweeter than honey to my mouth!
Psalm 119:103

Every time the Lord spoke to me, I eagerly wrote His words in my journal, pondered them, and turned the page. There they stayed.

Then I went through a dry spell when I didn't hear the Lord speak to me. Hungry, I waited before Him until gently He said, "I have already told you, but you have not taken heed." I went back to my journal, puzzled. What had I missed? There, to my dismay, in little pieces throughout my writings, He had revealed His vision of me.

Suddenly I grasped the import of my Creator's words. I saw that the power of His sweet words was not in writing them down, but in my taking them in. When they finally became a part of me, I changed.

Thank You, Lord, for freely giving Your word. Help me to receive Your words in my heart so that they can bring change in my life.

> *You shall not be afraid of the terror by night,*
> *Nor of the arrow that flies by day.*
>
> Psalm 91:5

The arrow is still in your heart," she said, "and it keeps you a victim." I didn't understand, but as I listened, the Lord taught me about arrows.

First, I had allowed the arrow into my heart. Second, I had let it stay there and each time I thought about it, it pierced deeper. Third, I could only remove it by forgiving the person who hurt me, giving God my bitterness, and inviting His gentle balm to heal my heart. Then the Lord encouraged me further: "It takes a lot more strength to pull an arrow out than it took to shoot it in!"

Obediently, I pulled. Waves of release swelled through me as Jesus washed over the wound and set my heart free!

Thank You for strengthening me, Lord, so that I don't have to stay a victim.

They are new every morning.
Lamentations 3:23

As we face the abuse that occurred, sometimes it seems that everything around us is shaded by the darkness of it. It's as if a veil has been pulled over our eyes and the sunshine can't push its way through. The word *seems* is important here. If we take some time to lift the veil, we can get a new perspective.

Picture the beauty of the morning as a painting God is creating for us; see the soft hues that He strokes with His brush. Sense the newness of the day as the sun rises and out of the darkness comes light. The brilliance grows, the same as God's love for you and me. God wants us to be enveloped in His love. Why not let Him share the sunrise of each morning? He promises to give us a brand new day, every day.

O, Lord, help me to come to You to start my days, for You are new every morning.

For I have satiated the weary soul, and I have replenished every sorrowful soul.

Jeremiah 31:25

Going through recovery has been draining and exhausting for me. People question me about my progress because I sometimes look worse, rather than better. They often give me advice or a few quick Bible verses to pick me up. Sometimes I get mad at their "helpful hints."

One day I had spent three hours in my counselor's office, remembering and praying through the trauma of my father molesting me. I was a weary and sorrowful soul. When my sister called me later at home, she lectured me about where I "should" be right now. She told me she thought I should be over this by now.

I napped for a few hours and awoke with the Lord on my mind. Then I read a psalm and prayed, "Lord, help me through this day." As I went about listening to praise music, He began to satiate and replenish my soul.

Lord, I am weary. Replenish my soul.

Their sorrow was turned into joy.
Esther 9:22 NIV

If we were to go into a store and see the joy of the Lord for sale, with the price being our years of sexual abuse, how many of us would be willing to pay the price? If we had never experienced the true joy of the Lord, our focus would be on the cost and not on the potential gift.

If we allow Him, God will take our years of sorrow and pain and exchange them for His joy. Allow Him to touch your life today.

Thank You, Father, for Your great mercy and loving-kindness. Help me to remember You can take any circumstance and turn it into joy.

HARD QUESTIONS

How could You simply stand aside,
You who hold power in Your hand,
or were You seated on Your throne,
high and lofty,
watching on
as she lay pinned against the floor?

What kind of Love are You
to hear her silent screams
and allow innocence
to be pierced through
while You wait
and evil plays
until it's done?

Tell me! Let me hear from You!
Answer me, and explain Your grace!
Where was justice?
How was goodness robed
as the hellish pleasure ravaged on,
carving terror and filth
into her young soul?

Look at me now
as You looked at me then,
and let me see Your holy eyes.
Did You cry? Did You feel the shame?
Within those wounds will You pour oil
to soothe the ragged raw of pain?

And will You hold a dirtied rose?
And will You heal the timeless "why?"

"Yes, child."

© Carlene Hacker

*We are hard pressed on every side, but not
crushed; perplexed, but not in despair;
persecuted, but not abandoned; struck
down, but not destroyed.*

2 Corinthians 4:8–9 NIV

There is an age-old question that comes from those abusive times—why? Like Job, we believe the answer would help us reconcile the horror. I recall looking into a seventy-two-year-old sister's troubled eyes as she asked, "Why?" Her birth parents had died when she was just a baby. In her adopted home, she had known nothing but abuse—physical, sexual, emotional.

I felt a scream well up inside of me. "Yeah, almighty, all-powerful God—why?" God reminded me that Job's release of that answer brought the deep comforting love of a Father who never abandoned him. Our Father promises to heal us and vindicate us of the most horrendous acts done against us.

Oh, dear God, help us to hold tight to You as we try to make sense of the senseless. Help us to let go of the "why" so we can press into You.

> *When my father and my mother*
> *forsake me,*
> *Then the LORD will take care of me.*
>
> Psalm 27:10

God saw the fights and torment between my father and mother. He knew that the road ahead would be rocky for me. She left first; the struggle was just too much for her. "Mom," I cried out, "don't leave me. Please come back." But there was no answer. With each passing day my father grew more angry, more bitter. He beat me and soon he abandoned me, too.

Now I'm all alone. I have no father, no mother. Will the pain ever go away? My tears flow like rivers before the Lord. Tenderly He receives me, holds me in His arms, and dries my tears. The pain stops as He says to me, "I will take care of you. Come to me."

Thank You for adopting me, Lord, after my mother and father had forsaken me.

> *For You are with me;*
> *Your rod and Your staff,*
> *they comfort me.*
> Psalm 23:4

Once the horror subsided, I realized Jesus was there protecting me. I was the little lost sheep and He was the Good Shepherd. He came into my darkness and now the rod of His Word defends me against the enemies of fear and shame. He comforts me with His staff (His Spirit) and draws me to Him.

His Word tells me He will never leave me or forsake me (see Heb. 13:5); He has called me by my name and I am His (see Isa. 43:1). I know His voice, and I will not follow the voice of another (see John 10:4). His Spirit is ever present to comfort me in my pain (see John 14:26) and take away all my fear (see Ps. 34:4).

Jesus, You are my Good Shepherd. I trust You to take care of me and my past.

> *Talk no more so very proudly; let no arrogance*
> *come from your mouth, for the Lord is the God*
> *of knowledge; and by Him actions are weighed.*
> 1 Samuel 2:3

This verse is taken from the motherly prayer of Hannah. Hannah had vowed that if God gave her a son she would give him back to the Lord. Her heart was rejoicing, but it was hard for her to give her son over for the priest to raise. Here she declares that the Lord is the God of knowledge who weighs every man's actions. She knows He will watch over her son.

I was an abandoned child. The Lord watched over me even though I was unaware of Him. He was very aware of the actions of my abusers against me. I know He has weighed their actions and will bring justice.

Lord, I surrender to You my need for justice. Weigh the actions of those who have sinned against me and deal with them according to Your will.

Would not God search this out?
For He knows the secrets of the heart.

Psalm 44:21

Some women have always remembered their sexual abuse. Others have repressed it so deeply that they are not aware of it at all. In the beginning I did not know what was troubling me. I only knew that something down deep inside was wrong. I could not remember parts of my past. I had unexplained fear, anxiety, and uncontrollable anger. Where was it all coming from?

God knew! He knew every detail, all the secrets buried within me. One by one, He searched them out and showed them to me. Why? So that He could heal the torment of my past and set me free!

Open our hearts today, Lord, and search out the hidden secrets there so that we may be healed and set free.

> *For a righteous man may fall seven times and*
> *rise again.*
>   Proverbs 24:16

I think I see light at the end of the tunnel." "Great!" my counselor rejoiced. "Yes," I said, "except I'm afraid it might be a train." We laughed, but within two weeks the oncoming train thundered over me and reality came crashing in.

How many times, Lord, will I lay flattened in the middle of the tunnel just when I thought the end was in sight? Today's verse came to me in the darkness.

Yes, I would rise again as before—not by my own power, but by God giving me His courage and strength and even His desire that I continue this journey toward healing.

The road from devastation to recovery is not a quick trip down the expressway. No, this highway's markers are pain and anger, flashbacks and setbacks. But God promises that we will rise again from each obstacle and He empowers us to do so.

Lord, You assure me that this journey is worth the trouble by giving me Your strength to rise after each fall.

I was cast upon You from birth.
From My mother's womb
You have been My God.
Be not far from Me,
For trouble is near;
For there is none to help.

Psalm 22:10–11

The pressure on survivors of sexual abuse mounts as the nation gears up for Mother's Day. The beautiful cards contain poems extolling Mom's virtues with lines like "Mother, you were always there for me, understanding my pain." The little girl inside us still wants a mother who is all that these verses describe. Our pain intensifies each time we read cards we could never send home. For many of us, Mom was the source of our pain, not the comforter that others have known.

All that our mothers could not provide and more is available to us through the love and care of Jesus Christ. He took us up each time we were cast aside. His comforting arms waited for us each time our bodies experienced pain. In times of trouble, He made a way of escape for us.

Jesus, be not far from me as I face the pain of Mother's Day.

> *But we were gentle among you, just as a*
> *nursing mother cherishes her own children.*
> 1 Thessalonians 2:7

I can't remember, though I've tried hard. "Please, God, let me remember," I say over and over. I want to remember sitting on my mother's lap, reading a book about Cinderella; or going to the park and having her push me on a swing; or, better yet, nursing at her breast. I agonize and cry because the memories just aren't there.

I crave the gentle touch of my mother, holding me close and nurturing me. Someone to run to, cry on, and laugh with. But I have no memories, no feelings of nurture ever happening in the past.

But now God says He will be gentle. He will hold me and cherish me.

Ah . . . I'm starting over. I sit on His lap and read a book; go to the park and swing; and run up and cry on His breast. He pulls me close just as a nursing mother cherishes her babe.

Thank You, Lord, for being my mother.

*Visiting the iniquity of the fathers upon the
children and the children's children to the third
and the fourth generation.*   Exodus 34:7

The Hebrew word for iniquity means "twisted, distorted, warped, or perverted." As sexually abused women we have personally experienced the effects of distorted and warped views of sex.

Those of us who are mothers don't want to see our daughters experience this same pain and shame. We don't want to see our sons emulate their fathers or grandfathers in abusing and using women.

We need God's love and forgiveness to start the healing process, not only in ourselves but in our children, so that the iniquities of the fathers will no longer be passed down to future generations.

Thank You, Father, for showing us how necessary it is to be healed. Heal us so that our children may be healthy and whole.

> *Children's children are a crown to the aged and*
> *parents are the pride of their children.*
>
> Proverbs 17:6 NIV

What an abused woman will not do for herself she will do for her children. Her desire to keep them free of the generational ties of victimization can often spur the decision for change and healing. Use your concern for your children as an impetus for change.

Take time to see the children full of life, eyes sparkling with laughter and freely running into a warm embrace. Keep this picture in mind. It will help bring you strength to face the pain and establish a new heritage for all children. They will be victors instead of victims.

Dear Lord, it is difficult to face the pain. Thank You for giving us our children as strong reminders of our responsibility to break the patterns of the past. Let us be the pride of our children and let them be the crown to the aged.

So the Lord alone led him and there was no foreign god with him.   Deuteronomy 32:12

A foreign god, or idol, is anything other than God that controls us.

As children we learned to yield to the power of the abusers in order to have our basic needs met. As adults we continue to give men too much power in our lives for the same reason. They become our gods; our lives revolve around them. They consume our time and thoughts.

If we are to break out of this victim role, we must take our eyes off men and look to the Lord, giving Him the power we have previously given them.

As we yield to Him and enjoy the benefits of that surrender—the perfect meeting of our needs—He will lead us and there will be no idols in our lives.

Lord, remove my need for other gods in my life, for You alone satisfy.

And you are complete in Him.
Colossians 2:10

As abused and wounded women, we are often co-dependent and continue in unhealthy relationship patterns. Before we can begin to have healthy relationships with the people we care for, we must first find our value, our self-worth, and our identity in Christ.

To do this we must constantly go to Him and His Word for support. He wants us to know that we are deeply and completely loved by Him. He knows the evil of our hearts and still loves us as we are. We don't need to search for this love in other human beings when it is so completely available in Him.

We are complete in Him.

Father, help me to look to You for completeness, love, and fulfillment. May I learn to value myself as You value me.

*To know the love of Christ which passes
knowledge; that you may be filled with
all the fullness of God.*   Ephesians 3:19

As a survivor of sexual abuse, I have a tremendous
need for love and support. This need is so great it
sometimes feels like a bottomless pit. No matter
how much love and attention I receive, I always
crave more. This puts a strain on my relationships.
People are capable of giving only so much from
their resources of time, energy, and love.

But God's love is abundant. *God is love!* He has
unlimited time and energy to spend with me. He is
the only one who can fill the emptiness within me.

As I seek, accept, and am filled with His love, I
will have more love to give to others.

Father, please fill me with Your love today.

> *The Lord delights in those who fear Him,*
> *who put their hope in His unfailing love.*
>
> Psalm 147:11 NIV

The psalmist's words are so alive and infectious! The Lord delights in us and His love is unfailing. Many of us have never experienced an unfailing love here on earth and few of our relationships have been delightful.

Instead our lives have been filled with pain, loneliness, self-condemnation, and shame, just the opposite of our Father's plan for His creation. Place your hand in His today. Place your hope in His unfailing love and know the delight He will take in you if you will fear Him.

Thank You, Father, for giving us a love that never lets us down.

A happy heart makes the face cheerful,
but heartache crushes the spirit.

Proverbs 15:13 NIV

Have you ever looked into the smiling face and eyes of a child? Innocence and joy make them sparkle with excitement and life. God gifts each one of us with a unique personality, but life has a way of twisting, distorting, and crushing that God-given spirit.

We who have been abused know firsthand how the joy can be crushed. The smiles disappear and the eyes become downcast. But when we are broken there is someone to turn to. God is waiting for us. He can restore that broken, battered child within us. His touch can make that child bloom and grow. He can restore the joyful heart.

Father, help me to regain that joyful child You created me to be. Mend my broken spirit.

> *Now may our Lord Jesus Christ Himself, and*
> *our God and Father, who has loved us . . .*
> *comfort your hearts and establish you in every*
> *good word and work.*
>
> 2 Thessalonians 2:16–17

Sometimes I fear I am in desperate trouble. It surrounds me like a dark cloud, ever-present, threatening to gather me up into its raging storm of panic.

Like most abused women, I feel this way when there is something in my life beyond my control. I am reacting to the powerlessness I felt as a child.

Now I've learned to take my inner child, with her feelings of powerlessness, and crawl up into my heavenly Father's lap. I tell Him all about my fears and loss of control.

There He comforts and reassures me that He is the one in control of my life. I can rest in Him.

Thank You, Father, for Your love, comfort, and security.

He has sent Me to heal the brokenhearted, to preach deliverance to the captives and recovery of sight to the blind, to set at liberty those who are oppressed.   Luke 4:18

Jesus came to set us free from the prisons of our past and the bondages of the present. He is constantly moving us toward healing and deliverance as we are willing. When we examine our response to crisis in light of His healing, He will take us another step toward freedom.

One of my unrecognized responses was eating for comfort. After a painful confrontation my friend at work tried to comfort me. In the midst of tears I suggested a trip to the candy machine. With every swallow I grew calmer. I actually felt my emotions recede as the candy pushed them down. Before it was gone my tears were dry and I was in control again.

That was the first of a series of revelations that would lead me out of the captivity of never recognizing, expressing, or resolving my feelings. It was a step toward breaking the bondage of food in my life.

You were sent, Lord, to heal me. You know better than I what keeps me imprisoned and You know how to set me free. Show me, through my reactions, the next step in my healing and deliverance.

> *Death and life are in the power of the tongue.*
> Proverbs 18:21

For years I couldn't figure out why I got so upset hearing men make derogatory remarks about women, even in fun. It irritated something deep inside me.

One day I heard a very sensitive man say, "No man could ever know the emotional pain a woman feels as a victim of sexual abuse." It was then I realized I felt victimized whenever I heard those critical words. They provoked my shame and made me feel worthless as a woman, not valued and precious as Jesus sees me.

Father, help me to forgive men when they say hurtful or critical things about women. Let not their words provoke death in me.

I have seen his ways, and will heal him.
Isaiah 57:18

My jealousy burned. This was supposed to be our fun time at Grandma and Grandpa's house, but that cousin always ruined everything!

Actually, it was my own intense hatred that caused the fights and disagreements, behavior that thoroughly embarrassed me even years later as I recalled the memory. My cousin seemed to have everything I wanted and I envied her. The truth was she never had a father, became a mother at fifteen, and suffered three failed marriages.

My own abuse had clouded my vision and I was unable to see her pain. As abused women we tend to see our ways, not God's or others'.

Dear Father, heal my selfish ways. Open my eyes to the hurt of others. Let me see Your ways and healing.

And whenever you stand praying, if you have anything against anyone, forgive him, that your Father in heaven may also forgive you your trespasses.

Mark 11:25

We have passed on the wounds of abuse to our husbands, children, and friends. They have become victims of our victimization. We may have vowed that we would never let anyone take advantage of us again, closing off our hearts to others or flying into a rage any time we feel mistreated. Regrettably, the sin of our abuse gets passed on to those we love.

It is hard to have empathy for our abusers. But even as we have felt powerless to control ourselves, those who abused us may have felt just as trapped. Many of them were also victimized; knowing this can help us forgive. Our forgiveness of another allows God to determine the consequences of their sin. Only He can rightly judge their actions, motives, and past.

Lord, show me what I need to be forgiven for so that I may be encouraged to forgive my abusers.

> *I will remove from them their heart of stone and give them a heart of flesh.* Ezekiel 11:19 NIV

Survivors of sexual abuse reach a point in recovery where we must consciously choose to let go of the rage that holds us in bondage to our pain. Once we have dealt with the root of our anger we must let it go, or this now self-inflicted wound will take root in us, fester, and harden our hearts.

We must renounce our anger, along with the false guilt and worthlessness that reinforce it. We must ask God to remove our heart of stone and replace it with a heart of flesh—one in which the love and joy of His Spirit can be planted and grow.

Ask God to give you the faith and grace to let go so that He can transform your heart and life.

Lord, thank You for removing the stone in my heart and replacing it with flesh so that I can move on in my life, no longer tied to my pain.

> *Every branch in Me that does not bear fruit He*
> *takes away; and every branch that bears fruit*
> *He prunes, that it may bear more fruit.*
>
> John 15:2

Every gardener knows pruning encourages new growth. Pruning is usually done in the winter when the plant is at rest. Branches that are over a year old may bleed or ooze when cut. Some plants get trimmed back so severely they look like they may never bloom again.

As we recover from sexual abuse God does much pruning, cutting away the anger, fear, and resentments of our childhood. Often there is so much pain revealed that we wonder if we will ever recover.

Have faith! Just as the plants bloom again and bring forth new growth, we too will experience God's healing and bear new fruit in our lives.

Thank You, Lord, for loving me enough to prune away those areas in my life which do not produce fruit.

But the fruit of the Spirit is love, joy, peace, longsuffering, kindness, goodness, faithfulness, gentleness, self-control. Galatians 5:22–23

Have you ever gone into the grocery store and seen plump, delicious-looking, sweet-smelling fruit, but the cost was greater than you could afford or wanted to pay? So it is with the fruits of the Spirit. How many of us would offer to pay the price if God opened our eyes to the future and said, "This is what you must endure before you will obtain the fruits of the Spirit"?

Probably few of us would even acquire the first one by ourselves. We are too frail, afraid, and insecure on our own. But our Lord gently leads us, never leaving our side, and shows us only what we need to see in order to take the next step with Him. Working through our abuse ripens the fruits of the Spirit in our lives.

Father, it is my heart's desire to have the fruits of the Spirit, but I can gain them only with Your help.

> *I have come that they may have life, and that*
> *they may have it more abundantly.*
>
> John 10:10

Avoiding life often preoccupies women who have suffered sexual abuse. They avoid family gatherings, unfamiliar surroundings, and places where men are likely found. Sometimes they avoid leaving home if that's their safe place.

Jesus wants us to embrace life, not avoid it. He wants to break the power of our fears because He has plans for us. He designed life to have meaning and purpose and to include meaningful relationships. If we trust Him with our lives He will fulfill His plan. If we trust our fears we will never experience His plan for our lives.

Lord, help me overcome my fears and face life as an adventure we walk together.

> *But I will sing of Your power;*
> *Yes, I will sing aloud of Your mercy*
>   *in the morning;*
> *For You have been my defense*
> *And refuge in the day of my trouble.*
>
> Psalm 59:16

I'm ugly, frumpy, and forty. How could any man be interested in me?" Victims of sexual abuse often victimize themselves through neglect. Though they desire to have a man love and care for them, the thought of having sex can be overwhelming. So, they unconsciously build a defense around themselves by putting on weight, neglecting personal hygiene, or wearing mismatched, out-of-style clothing.

This type of defense is no guarantee against future abuse. It is only a sign of self-abuse. Jesus is a powerful defender and His ways are the only sure defense. He is our only refuge. In His mercy He will provide a way of healing and escape from our troubles.

Lord, help me to rest in the power of Your defense so that I might sing of Your mercies each morning.

*I can do all things through Christ who
strengthens me.*   Philippians 4:13

Until we are healed of our pasts, we who were sexually abused often nurture self-defeating ideas and self-inflicted limitations. We don't think we are worthy, capable, or talented. "Not good enough" is imprinted on our brains. We find it hard to believe that our lives can be anything but average, or below. We find it even harder to believe that we have talents that God wants to use. We have become pitiful products of our past abuse, put-downs, and lies.

Let us break out of this place by first inviting Him to show us His vision of who we are in Him. Next, let us reject our natural inclination to deny His vision as "too good to be true." Then let us take the risk of trusting God and allow Him to do *through* us, *in* us, and *with* us whatever He wants. We will be amazed at what we can do in Him.

Dear Jesus, strengthen my self-image and encourage me to do things I never thought possible.

Where the Spirit of the Lord is, there is liberty.
2 Corinthians 3:17

I trembled at the thought of having a date. My mind searched for excuses to put it off. "What's wrong with you?" my friends would ask. It would be a time of excitement for most girls.

But I remembered the fear all over again, the fear of my stepfather, standing in the shadows waiting to grab me. Even the sound of his voice used to make me cringe.

"God," I cried out, "I hate being a woman." Then a silence came over me. "My daughter," the voice of the Lord said, "I will repair the damage and give you freedom to smile, laugh, and be a whole woman."

Lord, continue to liberate me to rejoice in my womanhood.

> *I will seek what was lost and bring back what
> was driven away, bind up the broken and
> strengthen what was sick.*   Ezekiel 34:16

I watched as the tears flowed. She said, "My heart is broken." The pain was pouring out. She continued, "I see God holding me—or is it really me?" Then she realized it was her as a child. She cried harder as the little girl told of the horror. The adult was filled with grief. "O God, help her!"

All at once, she seemed to go limp; all was quiet. I waited. She said God lifted the little girl into His arms and drew her to His breast. A jolt ran through her as she realized He was healing the adult and the little girl at the same time. No longer would she be a shell broken apart in two pieces. She had been a fractured person because of all the abuse, but because she was willing to allow God into those painful places, He put her back together.

Lord, make me willing to face my pain. You can bind up what was broken and strengthen what was sick.

> *Take heed to yourselves. If your brother sins*
> *against you, rebuke him; and if he repents,*
> *forgive him.*
>   Luke 17:3

Forgiveness has not come easily since I've been on the road to recovery. This may seem paradoxical. Yet when I confessed it to the Lord, He showed me that some of us have been *too* quick to forgive.

We have forgiven everybody for everything. We have accepted the blame when we weren't to blame, we've received shame when it wasn't our shame, we've changed when we didn't need to change, we've believed that lie that it's all our fault. We've never thought enough of ourselves to say, "No, you're wrong."

As I dealt with the issues of sexual abuse, I became more aware of myself as a person—God's creation, formed by Him with valid needs and ideas, gifts and desires. Abuse no longer intimidated me.

To forgive blindly is victim behavior. To confront in a spirit of forgiveness leads us to victory.

Teach me, Lord, to think enough of myself to confront abusive behavior before I automatically forgive it.

> *Search me, O God, and know my heart;*
> *Try me, and know my anxieties;*
> *And see if there is any wicked way in me,*
> *And lead me in the way everlasting.*
>
> Psalm 139:23–24

I like to pray this Scripture now and then. It's like getting a spiritual checkup.

God knows me better than I know myself. This Scripture prayer began my journey to unlock the sexual abuse in my past. It wasn't easy, but I'm better for it. I have learned many things about my past and myself that I didn't understand before.

Sometimes I'm afraid to think what else God may show me about myself, but I would rather know and be healed than have it remain hidden. I know that I can trust Him to be gentle and always do what is best for me.

Search me, O God, and lead me in Your way.

*Now thanks be to God, who always leads us in
triumph in Christ, and through us diffuses the
fragrance of His knowledge in every place.*
2 Corinthians 2:14

The journey of healing is long. But be assured it
ends triumphantly in a song, for along the road
seeds are planted in our hearts. Watered and tenderly cared for, they grow, blossom, and bloom.

One day, as we travel through life, the garden
within can no longer be contained. From out of our
mouths flow sweet fragrant flowers, love songs
rooted deep in our hearts for the One who has
walked each step alongside us, our constant companion, our God.

His presence has changed us. Our lives tell the
story, and others are moved by our song. They experience His grace and start their own journey,
hands tucked safe in His own. He plants in their
hearts those small seeds of faith that grow as they
travel along.

*Thank You, Lord. Because of my triumphant journey in You,
others will know the fragrance of Your love.*

A CHILD'S JOURNEY

She lay in helpless agony,
the sweat and heave of human flesh
upon her.
She was a child,
soft and tender,
used by man,
bathed in her own blood and vomit,
and left unclean.

Into the nakedness of that truth,
You brought me,
as if drawn through
the eye of a needle,
a woman rich in error and lies,
now made poor
by the sight of a child.

You wore no royal robes.
There was no scepter in Your hand,
no magic to remove the shame
and pronounce her, "Whole."
You knew I'd accept no such grandeur,
no slick touch or lifeless word.
This was too real, too deep
for smiles or pretense,
though I wanted You
to wave a wand, to take this pain.

You had.
It took time
for me to know it,
time to feel the fervor
of a thousand thunderous storms,
the wash of unrelenting rain,
living now what a child
could not then.
You knew it,
and I knew Your greatness,
gracing me with love.

In time,
through that forgotten horror.
I saw You, full
with the violation of my hell.
Yet You held more,
bowing low
to intercourse with human ways.

Here was a God
who was not too small,
amid the dung and knowable,
reachable, reaching
to take a child's hand.

*And do not be conformed to this world, but be
transformed by the renewing of your mind,
that you may prove what is that good and
acceptable and perfect will of God.*

Romans 12:2

As the sense of being trapped engulfed me and the
need to escape overpowered me, I could feel my
mind slipping off into a deep sleep. I fought against
the drowsiness, my conscious mind battling my
subconscious. I did not need this means of self-
protection anymore. The Lord had shown me I had
other choices. I was no longer a victim. With His
help, I could change my tendency to shut down.

Victims of sexual abuse struggle with feeling
trapped. When our bodies were literally trapped
during the acts of abuse, we found various ways of
escape. Shutting down and turning off was mine. As
adults we continue to use our childhood coping de-
vices until we become aware of them and choose to
change.

Change can sometimes be scary and unsettling,
but the battle is worth the reward—living in the perfect will of God.

---

*Lord, I welcome the changes You are making in me. Renew my
mind.*

> *And God is able to make all grace abound*
> *toward you, that you . . . have an abundance*
> *for every good work.*　　2 Corinthians 9:8

Often my mind was preoccupied with tormenting questions. Could these memories really be true? Did the abuse really happen? It was easier to think it didn't, but I could not ignore the facts. I could never trust any man to come close to me, and my personal life was a disaster. "Lord, help me," I wept. He responded tenderly, "I have grace for you, child. Go on with your work toward healing."

As God encourages us to look back in our pasts and sort through the memories, He dispels our doubts and renews our courage. Let us confidently pursue the good work of our healing in the abundance of His grace.

Thank You, Lord, for Your abundant grace to me as I worked toward my healing.

*The Spirit Himself bears witness with our spirit
that we are children of God, and if children,
then heirs.* Romans 8:16–17

If I was ever going to get well, I knew I had to talk
about the sexual abuse. I had to break the secrecy
code under which I had grown up. Dysfunctional
families share the code: "Don't trust, don't feel,
don't talk"—all in the name of family loyalty. In order to heal, I had to risk my family's rejection and
reveal family secrets.

When I finally believed my worth in God's eyes, I
was able to take the risk and break the code. I
switched my loyalty to God, believing that I was His
child and had all the rights that come with that position.

We must recognize that family loyalty perpetu-
ates our family's sickness. Loyalty to our heavenly
Father starts us on the road to health.

Thank You, Father, that as Your heir I can be healthy.

> *But you received the Spirit of adoption by whom
> we cry out, "Abba, Father." The Spirit Himself
> bears witness with our spirit that we are
> children of God.*　　　Romans 8:15–16

These horrible things keep whirling around my
head. Why do I see my daddy's face? He was so
kind, so fun. He would never allow anyone to do
bad things to me. But I remember him saying, "I
love you. This may hurt you, but I love you. I only do
this to those I love most. You're so special, my special little girl." I'm so confused. I don't understand. I
don't feel special; I feel used and abused.

Somewhere deep inside now I hear. "Yes, it was
your daddy who hurt you. But I'm not like him. I will
never violate you and make you feel dirty. I will love
you for you. I will heal you, not hurt you."

---

*Father God, help me to remember I need not fear You. You are
not like my daddy. You are "Abba, Father."*

*Let love be without hypocrisy. Abhor what is
evil. Cling to what is good.*
                                        Romans 12:9

He was sick!" I told myself over and over. How
could anyone do to a small child the things he had
done to me, unless he was mentally ill? *He* was my
father, and I refused to see him as a wicked man.
My brokenness, however, was undeniable. I knew
deep inside that I could never reclaim my life until I
stopped defending his crimes and explaining away
the damage.

As I counted the cost of clinging to my excuses, I
saw that it was not my responsibility to protect my
father's character. My walls of fear melted away, ex-
posing my anger, and God began to heal me.

When the perpetrator is also our father, love gets
distorted. We think we can only love him by pre-
tending it didn't happen or making excuses for him.
When we face reality, abhor the evil, and cling to
God's goodness, we will learn to love in truth.

Lord, heal my distortions of love.

When I was a child, I spoke as a child, I
understood as a child, I thought as a child;
but when I became a [woman], I put away
childish things.   1 Corinthians 13:11

An important part of recovery is the process of uncovering and dismantling the lies and misbeliefs that come from being victimized as a child. I can't continue to think like a victimized child. Now I clearly understand that what happened to me was not my fault. I did not deserve it; I did not cause it; I was not responsible for it. The shame that my child-like thinking had accepted was not mine either.

The Lord has renewed my thinking and my understanding, and I have been able to put away the childish accusations against me that once I so readily believed.

Just today, Lord, please help me put away childish things. Begin to reveal and change the lies I have accepted about myself and others.

Honor thy father.
Ephesians 6:2 KJV

How do you honor a man who has sexually, physically, and emotionally abused you? How do you join in the family traditions on Father's Day and birthdays? Many of us have suffered in silence, giving cards and gifts like everyone else in the family so no one will know of our secret pain. As adults it becomes harder to keep silent and play the role of the loving daughter, so we wrestle with the commandment to "honor thy father."

We can show honor by showing respect for the office or position a person holds, even if the person's behavior does not warrant respect. To honor does not mean to deal falsely; the truth is what sets us free. Jesus may be asking us to confront our fathers respectfully about the truth of their abuse. In doing so we may find a response we are able to honor.

Lord, help me find a way to keep Your commandment to honor my father.

*For you did not receive the spirit of bondage
again to fear, but you received the Spirit of
adoption by whom we cry out, "Abba, Father."*
Romans 8:15

He grabbed my shoulder and shook me with impatience, saying, "Didn't you hear me?" "No," I responded truthfully. I had slipped into my other person, a happy little girl playing in a meadow of peace and safety. I was in a place where I could say, "Go away!" and my father could not hurt me.

Now, years later, I'm being introduced to another Father. I sink in fear, for I assume a new father means new pain. "Not so," my friends tell me, "for God our Father is love."

Those of us who were molested by our fathers find it especially hard to accept God the Father without fear. But our Father in heaven is not a copy of our fathers on earth; rather, He is to be their model. We can count on Him to be the "Abba" we always wanted. In His loving protection we will find healing and wholeness.

Thank You, my Father, for making me whole in mind and heart.

But Jesus said, "Let the little children come to Me, and do not forbid them."

Matthew 19:14

Focus on Me, dear child. Climb up into My arms and do not be afraid. Let Me comfort and reassure you. Put your head on My shoulder and let My arms shelter you. There is nothing to fear."

Doesn't that sound like a lovely place to be when we are scared or sad or hurt? At those times we little girls need to climb up in our Father's lap. As He comforts and reassures us, we find rest and peace in His arms. His love surrounds us and we rejoice as He delights in us, His little children.

When at last we reluctantly climb down, His parting words go with us, "All is well, my daughter—better than ever."

Thank You, Jesus, for welcoming me in Your arms when my little girl needs comfort. I always climb down rejoicing!

> *Let the little children come to Me, and do not*
> *forbid them; for of such is the kingdom of God.*
> Luke 18:16

Jesus loves the little girl in me! At first, I had trouble accepting my inner child and wanted to ignore her completely. But sometimes it felt like there were two of me: the person on the outside in the real world and the child deep inside who was still a frightened victim.

As long as I ignored this child's pain I could not be whole. I had to acknowledge her and allow her to speak. In learning to care for her, I began to learn how to take care of the whole me.

Jesus wants to love and heal our inner children. He wants us to be well and whole.

Jesus, help me surrender to You, and allow the little girl in me to come to You.

Jesus wept.
John 11:35

Jesus wept over a city. He wept at the tomb of His friend. Why would He not weep over us?

Asking God why He had allowed my abuse was a turning point for me. As I prayed for an answer, I remembered a painful scene. This time, however, the Lord was standing next to my abuser as he began attacking me. The Lord called his name, commanding him to stop. Repeatedly He admonished my attacker not to hurt me, but he was deaf to the Lord's voice, and Jesus wept.

I wept, too, for then I knew that my abuse was not the will of God, but the will of a man.

Thank You, Jesus, for understanding my pain and for weeping over me.

> *Yes, I have loved you with an everlasting love;*
> *Therefore with lovingkindness I have drawn you.*
>
> Jeremiah 31:3

Times of abuse are wounds to our heart, but His tender loving-kindness will heal them.

As one woman thought of her wounds, her tears silently fell down her cheeks. She was barely audible as she said, "My heart is too shattered, it can't be fixed." We prayed as she physically lifted her arms to Him, symbolically handing her broken heart to her healer. I sat holding my breath, finally whispering, "Can you tell me what's happening?" She looked up with awe, "The Lord showed me my heart couldn't be mended, so He reached in Himself and gave me His!" I hugged her, and we clung together with tears of rejoicing.

Dear Lord, help me know there is no heart so shattered that Your loving-kindness cannot restore it.

Rejoice in the Lord always. Again I will say, rejoice!
                                    Philippians 4:4

Paul tells us to rejoice and give thanks in all situations. To the wounded this sounds absurd. How can we possibly rejoice and give thanks in the difficult situations many of us face?

As we come to know our Lord more intimately we learn that God does turn the worst into something good. We can find joy by finding the silver lining in every situation. Then we will see that God uses every experience in our lives to accomplish His ultimate purpose.

Father, thank You for using all things in my life for Your glory. Just today, Lord, may I rejoice in my circumstances.

This people I have formed for Myself;
They shall declare My praise.

Isaiah 43:21

Imagine! I was formed for my Lord! He had a purpose and place for me before I was born. He chose the family I would be born into at His chosen time. And on the day I was born all heaven danced and rejoiced, because I was just what He made me to be.

He allowed my family's problems and turned the abuse into a blessing, for through it I came to know Him. Then I had a reason to praise.

God has formed you for Himself. He has a purpose and place for you, and as you yield to Him, He will use your experiences to fulfill the plan He has just for you. Let us joyously declare His praise!

O Lord, You formed me for Yourself. May my praise be a blessing to You.

> *But thanks be to God, who gives us the victory*
> *through our Lord Jesus Christ.*
>
> 1 Corinthians 15:57

We all have relapses during our healing. There are times when our buttons are pushed, our automatic responses are triggered, and we find ourselves in a victim role. Catching ourselves in old behavior patterns, we wonder when we'll ever change.

"But thanks be to God," relapses are normal. They are part of the process and they can be turned into victory. In them, God opens up a new part of us for examination. He reveals an attitude in need of change, a habit to be broken, an old tape that needs to be rewritten, a lie that we have believed.

Instead of signaling failure, a relapse can be an opportunity for God to heal. It becomes a springboard to further growth and greater freedom in Christ.

Thank You, Jesus, that You redeem even my relapses by showing me where I still need healing and by leading me to new growth.

Be still, and know that I am God.
Psalm 46:10

Sometimes I feel so out of touch with life around me. When I wake up I feel emotionally and mentally numb. I can only go through the motions of my day.

Realizing that every day cannot be a mountain-top experience, I have learned to accept these times in the valley. As I read the Word, pray, and write in my journal, I quietly listen to my inner child, to my feelings, and to the Spirit of God.

By being still and knowing God, I grow more in touch with myself and life around me.

Father, increase my capacity for being still and for knowing You.

*The hand of the LORD came upon me and
brought me out in the Spirit of the LORD,
and set me down in the midst of the valley;
and it was full of bones.*   Ezekiel 37:1

Maybe you have heard of the valley of dry bones
before but have wondered just what it was. In Ezekiel's vision, the valley represented the world, and
the dry bones represented the Jewish people, who
were scattered through the world without any hope
of a land of their own. God showed Ezekiel that
someday the Jewish people would come back to Israel. Fifty years later King Cyrus permitted the Jewish people to return to Palestine. And in recent
times many more have emigrated, making Israel a
nation in 1948.

Sexual abuse can cause victims to feel hopeless
and displaced, just as the Jewish people felt. I felt
abandoned and scattered like dry bones, having no
place to belong. But I heard God's promise to me
that someday I would belong. Have you also been
wandering in a valley of dry bones? God is calling
you to come back.

*Lord, by Your Spirit, bring me out of the valley of dryness into a
place of belonging.*

> *I will praise You, for I am fearfully*
> *and wonderfully made;*
> *Marvelous are Your works,*
> *And that my soul knows very well.*
>
> Psalm 139:14

Victims of abuse struggle with negative feelings about their bodies. Perhaps we have associated our bodies with sin, powerlessness, or even pain and shame. But God wants us to remember that our bodies are temples of His Holy Spirit, that they are His creation and He considers them clean, good, and acceptable.

Rejection of who we are physically is one of the blocks to our healing and recovery. When we truly embrace and accept our bodies we are in agreement with God. We need to make a conscious decision, sometimes daily, to accept our bodies.

Just today, carry an attitude of appreciation and gratitude about the specialness of your body in all its uniqueness. It is a gift of His love and an example of the miracle of His creation.

O Lord, help me to accept without reservation the body You have given me, for I am fearfully and wonderfully made.

Purge me with hyssop, and I shall be clean;
Wash me, and I shall be whiter than snow.
Psalm 51:7

Our sexuality sets us apart from all of creation. Unlike that of the animal kingdom, our sexuality exists for more than procreation. God has given us the capacity to feel fantastic depths of pleasure, joy, and oneness in sexual union. Our Creator planned for sex to be experienced in a marriage with God at its center. Many, however, have corrupted the gift of sex. They've selfishly used, abused, and demeaned others through its power.

Don't reject God's gift because of what a man has done. Don't reject your own sexuality. Allow God's love to touch, cleanse, and heal you. He will wipe away the past and make you new in Him.

Father, wash me and make me new again. Restore my innocence, removing all things from memory that would spoil my sexuality.

> *Let nothing be done through selfish ambition or conceit, but in lowliness of mind let each esteem others better than himself.* Philippians 2:3

We can be selfish so easily, even without realizing it. For many abused women, masturbation is their sin of selfishness.

God created Eve and Adam for each other, and they became one through physical pleasure. If God had intended Adam to fulfill and pleasure himself, then He would not have given him Eve.

Having lowliness of mind and esteeming our spouse is easier said than done, but we must communicate and work for harmony in our relationship. Then physical pleasure becomes true intimacy and not just having sex.

Lord, help me to control my selfish ambition, and esteem my husband.

> *"Comfort, yes, comfort My people!"*
> *says your God.*   Isaiah 40:1

We who have received healing can offer hope and comfort to others. God's healing power is like a mighty river flowing downstream. Its water nurtures the seeds He plants within our wounded souls. Over time the seeds grow, bringing a harvest of healing that we can sow into another's life.

"Praise be to the God and Father of our Lord Jesus Christ, the Father of compassion and the God of all comfort, who comforts us in all our troubles, so that we can comfort those in any trouble with the comfort we ourselves have received from God. . . . And our hope for you is firm, because we know that just as you share in our sufferings, so also you share in our comfort" (2 Cor. 1:3–4, 7 NIV).

Thank You, Lord, for Your comfort. As You give me opportunities, I will share Your comfort with others.

> *Whenever I am afraid,*
> *I will trust in You.*
> Psalm 56:3

I couldn't believe how scared I was. I had come so far in my healing, I thought I was beyond all that. But the fear had returned. As I confessed my chagrin to the Lord, He explained that although my mind knew all was well, the little girl within me still trembled at the thought of offending someone.

As adults we often repress fear, seeing it as a break in our faith. Actually it may be a breakthrough in our healing if we will just press into God.

We need to climb into our Father's arms and let Him show us the root of our fears. As we share them with the Lord, we receive the blessing of His comfort and another measure of healing.

Lord, give me the courage to trust You with my fear. What You reveal, You heal.

*For your Father knows the things you have need
of before you ask Him.*   Matthew 6:8

Our Father sees our future and, knowing what we
need, He equips us for it. As victims, however, we
think that things happen to us and we have no control. Thus, the moment of crisis may find us crying,
"Why me? Why did You let this happen, God?" We
are unaware that He has already provided us well in
advance with perfect tools.

God's Word is a tool we can use. It prepares us in
countless ways to face whatever the future brings. It
frees us from fear and guilt, changes our thought
patterns, rebuilds our self-esteem, corrects our
image of God, fills our needs for love and security,
and gives us hope and a plan for our future.

Let's not wait until the last minute to ask God for
help. Let's learn to use the tool He has already given
us.

——————————

*Thank You, Lord, that You have provided Your Word as the tool I
need to face the future. Teach me how to use it.*

> *The thief does not come except to steal, and to kill, and to destroy.*
>
> John 10:10

When we walk in obedience to the Lord, He blesses us with the delights of our hearts.

I had just returned from a much-needed weekend of relaxation in the mountains. Praising God for such a delightful treat, I turned on my answering machine only to learn of the death of a friend. Immediately I felt guilty. I had been enjoying myself, while my friend's family had been gathered around his deathbed.

Fortunately I was far enough along in my healing to recognize the enemy. God had blessed me, knowing full well what would happen while I was away, and Satan was trying to lay a guilt trip on me. I stopped and thanked God again for the refreshing weekend that had prepared me for the trials ahead.

Thank You, Lord, for helping me remember that when Satan tries to steal my blessings, I do not have to fall prey to his tricks.

*And He said, "Abba, Father, all things are
possible for You. Take this cup from Me;
nevertheless, not what I will, but what
You will."*

Mark 14:36

Pain often comes in waves; sometimes it bites so
sharply it takes your breath away. It may be physical pain or the emotional pain of rejection, a lost
childhood, or a fearful future. We cry out, "O Lord,
help me. I have nowhere to turn but to You. Lift this
pain from me."

Jesus prayed like this in the garden, crying out to
His heavenly Father. His pain was so agonizing He
sweat blood. Nevertheless, He endured the pain for
the joy set before Him.

He endured the pain for us then and feels our pain
now. It is His will that we face the bitter cup of our
pain and resolve it. He will sustain us through it. We
are but to fix our eyes on Him and yield only to Him,
not to our pain.

*Father, all things are possible for you. Take away this bitter cup of
pain from me; nevertheless, if I must face it to be healed, help me
keep my eyes fixed on You and not on my pain.*

> *O Lord, You have searched me and known me.*
> *You know my sitting down and my rising up;*
> *You understand my thought afar off.*
> *You . . . are acquainted with all my ways.*
>
> Psalm 139:1–3

God desires our healing, but we obstruct Him when we are afraid to speak honestly to Him and reveal our real thoughts and feelings. We often think if He finds out our true feelings He'll be mad, disappointed, or condemning.

We don't have to keep our masks on before Him. God already understands how we feel and why we feel. God never tells us not to feel—people do that. God does not drive us to unrealistic goals of perfection—we do that. We must not try to resolve all our negative feelings before praying to Him. We need only share our hearts with Him, and He'll help us with the feelings.

———————

Today, Father, free me from wrong perceptions of You and wrong expectations of me. You know me, understand me, and love me, negative feelings and all.

*I will give you a new heart and put a new
spirit within you.*   Ezekiel 36:26

My friend had just called to tell me that she had
been delivered from major problems, some of the
same problems with which I was still struggling. I
felt so discouraged. "What is wrong with me, Lord?"
I despaired. "I know that You could speak the word
and I would be healed. Why don't You? Why do I
always have to work through the attitudes of my
heart?"

His still voice answered my cry. "But child, I'm
changing your heart. I have a purpose and a plan for
you. Do not despair. I have hidden you in the palm
of My hand and you are forever before Me."

Contrary to how we sometimes feel, God never
forgets us; we are always in His hand. Although God
heals each of us differently, His purpose remains the
same—to give us new hearts and spirits, that we
might fulfill His plan for us.

Father, thank You for changing my heart—Your way.

> *Trust in the Lord with all your heart,*
> *And lean not on your own understanding.*
>
> Proverbs 3:5

Although she seemed slow, the white heifer with long ears tugged at my heart and I bought her. By the time we got home however, it was obvious the calf was very sick. Within five days, she was dead. Afterwards I agonized, saying, "Lord, I don't understand." The pain that little calf suffered without ever getting well had shaken me. I felt resigned to a similar fate.

Suddenly I remembered the day, years before, when I had accepted the lie that my life would always be one of suffering and pain like that poor sickly animal. God showed me how He had yearned to bless me all those years, but I had vowed instead to live the lie of hopelessness. God wept with me as I renounced my judgment.

Lord, as I trust You in every situation You help me understand Your purpose.

Being confident of this very thing, that He who has begun a good work in you will complete it until the day of Jesus Christ. Philippians 1:6

I can keep going for now, as long as I remember that it was God who began the healing in my life. He has brought me this far in the process and is responsible for seeing me through to the end! That thought is so freeing. When I start believing I must try to heal my aching heart by myself, I get overwhelmed. This job is way over my head.

I will keep in mind that all my attempts to go around my pain or over it or under it have been unsuccessful. The only way to relieve myself is to go through the pain. It is comforting to know that God will be right beside me along the way.

Lord, help me leave the work in Your hands so You can lead me through the pain.

> *I press toward the goal for the prize of*
> *the upward call of God in Christ Jesus.*
>
> Philippians 3:14

When life has been difficult, it's easy to escape into our longing for heaven, with its peace and security. However, recovery requires that we press on and escape no more.

We need to grasp the bits and pieces of eternity that God shows us today—the tinge of excitement, sparkle of love, and gifts of beauty.

Dear Lord, help me to embrace the gifts of life, looking forward to heaven but not being obsessed with it.

FRIENDS

I

Stand back, friend!
I need space to see the truth,
the raping twisted and denied.
I've known the fog of unreality
far too long,
and long now for the sun
to expose its lies.

You offer truth on a gilded plate,
as if sweets will solve
the hunger of a seeking heart
while syrupy words
only stick in my mouth.

I pray your attempt
to minimize my pain
will speak to you,
for I am angered
that your trust of my faith
in a giant-sized God
is so small.

II

Oh, my silent Friend,
Lover of my tormented soul,
Giver of no small answers,
I believe You're here,
standing in the shadows,
while I plumb the depths of pain,
not to watch me wallow,
as if to seek delight in misery.
You believe in me enough
to offer treasures
found only in dark places.

© Carlene Hacker

> *I will uphold you with My righteous right hand.*
> *You hold me by my right hand.*
>
> Isaiah 41:10; Psalm 73:23

If the Lord's right hand and my right hand are joined, we can't possibly be standing side by side. In order for Him to be upholding my right hand with His right hand, He must be reaching out to me. Actually, I think He is reaching down to take hold of me. Do you see the picture I see? My right arm is outstretched. I'm crying out:

> *Save me, O God!*
> *For the waters have come to my neck.*
> *I sink in deep mire,*
> *Where there is no standing;*
> *I have come into deep waters,*
> *Where the floods overflow me.*
> *I am weary with my crying. . . .*
> *I waited patiently for the LORD;*
> *And He inclined to me,*
> *And heard my cry.*
> *He also brought me up out of*
> *a horrible pit,*
> *Out of the miry clay,*
> *And set my feet upon a rock,*
> *And established my steps.*
>
> (Pss. 69:1–3; 40:1–2)

Thank You, Lord, for hearing my cries and for upholding me with Your righteous right hand.

I have called you friends.
John 15:15

As a child I was very sad and lonely. I tried to tell the grown-ups about the awful things that were happening to me, but no one ever heard me. I took comfort in an imaginary playmate, a friend who would never hurt me and who would always understand what I was trying to say.

Later I outgrew my imaginary friend, but I was still lonely. Eventually I became acquainted with "a friend who sticks closer than a brother" (Prov. 18:24). While my first friend was a creation of my own imagination, my second friend, Jesus, is quite real. He is my most comforting and understanding friend. He always listens and cares.

Because we've been abused we often feel alone inside. We need a real friend that will stick by us through thick and thin. We need Jesus.

Jesus, I desperately need a friend. Help me develop a friendship with You.

> *In You, O LORD, I put my trust;*
> *Let me never be put to shame. . . .*
> *For You are my hope, O Lord GOD;*
> *You are my trust from my youth.*
> Psalm 71:1, 5

When children are abused, trust becomes a problem. It's unbearable to acknowledge that the man who pushed you on the swings and gave you birthday presents is also the man who sexually abused you. Many young girls try to tell someone, only to be told that they must be mistaken. The people we trusted betrayed us.

Survivors of sexual abuse tend to see trust as an absolute; either they don't trust at all, or they trust completely. We may bounce between the two extremes, not trusting anyone until we are so desperate for contact that we throw our trust at the first likely target.

We need to remember that God will not abuse the trust we place in Him. We can put all our hope and trust in Him.

Father, help us to learn to trust You in everything. Give us the wisdom to know who to trust among men.

> *You have feared continually every day*
> *Because of the fury of the oppressor. . . .*
> *But I am the Lord your God. . . .*
> *And I have put My words in your mouth.*
> Isaiah 51:13, 15–16

Freedom! We're the most fortunate nation in the world, living for so long in freedom from the tyranny of others.

Just as our country fought for its independence many years ago and won the right to rule itself, so we must fight a personal battle to be free from the effects of the abuse we have suffered.

God's love empowers us to seek freedom from our longtime fear of men. He comforts us and strengthens us to undertake the journey to healing. Along the way, He delivers us from the fury and oppression under which we have lived. He instills in us a new self-worth based on who He says we are. He puts His words in our mouths and makes us bold in His truth.

Let us celebrate our personal freedom on this Independence Day!

Lord, thank You for delivering me from the fear of my oppressor, setting me free to be me!

*The Spirit of the L*ORD *shall rest upon Him,*
The Spirit of wisdom and understanding,
The Spirit of counsel and might,
The Spirit of knowledge and of the fear
   *of the L*ORD.

Isaiah 11:2

It would probably be less painful to stay in the dark about our sexual abuse than to face it, recognize its destructive force in our lives, and work toward healing and wholeness. However, once the Spirit gives us wisdom, throwing light into the darkness, it is difficult to ignore the truth.

Do we want to stay troubled and incomplete, or do we desire to become all that our heavenly Father created us to be? The choice is ours.

Our loving Father has promised not only wisdom and understanding but also His counsel and His strength to carry us through. He has thought of everything.

_____

May Your Spirit continue to rest on me, Father, as I struggle with the truths I am learning. Grant me Your wisdom and strength as I work toward becoming whole.

> *My voice You shall hear in the morning,*
> *O Lord;*
> *In the morning I will direct it to You,*
> *And I will look up.*   Psalm 5:3

The thought of facing a new day can be overwhelming. The prospect of enduring another day of painful struggling is enough to keep most of us in bed!

The secret to defeating this sense of dread is to bring our first thoughts immediately to the Lord. Sharing our feelings with Him and confessing our fears to Him in the morning unburdens us for the day ahead.

By lifting our voices to Him, we overcome all that would keep us downcast. By looking up, we look beyond ourselves and our circumstances and we see Him. When we fix our thoughts on Him, we gain the peace and assurance we need to face the new day.

> *I will lift up my eyes to the*
> *hills—*
> *From whence comes my help?*
> *My help comes from the LORD,*
> *Who made heaven and earth.*
> (Ps. 121:1–2)

*So He said, "Come." And when Peter had come
down out of the boat, he walked on the water to
go to Jesus.*   Matthew 14:29

As I walk through my healing I am breaking the
chains that kept me bound in the past—insecurities
and fears that led me to believe my value was based
on my performance, my ability to be perfect, and
my skill in "not rocking the boat."

Freedom began when I realized that the people
most insistent about keeping the boat of life steady
are those who are the most fearful. They mistak-
enly define a rocking boat as a sinking boat, and a
sinking boat means losing everything. They try to
control the boat and everyone in it, convinced they
have it all together.

Let us obey Jesus' command to come. Let us get
out of the boat, keep our eyes on Him, and walk into
freedom and wholeness.

*Thank You, Lord, for encouraging me to get out of the boat in-
stead of spending my life in a never-ending struggle to keep it
steady.*

> *In Him was life, and the life was the light*
> *of men.*
>
> John 1:4

Some victims of ongoing sexual abuse survive the years of trauma by creating other selves in order to cope. Several such personalities in me were revealed during the counseling process.

One day the sad, distant little girl who never speaks came out. "Hi," my counselor said. "Would you like to talk today?" Back and forth her head moved slowly, *No.*

"Okay, then come and sit right here." The little girl obeyed and the counselor put her arm around her shoulders, pulled her near and began to sing songs of Jesus. Deep inside some gentle traces of life stirred. As the songs continued, the girl became fully alive, alive to a world she had shut out long ago.

The only way we can ever become completely whole is by allowing Jesus to fill us with the light of life. Jesus is life in all its fullness. Let us allow His songs of love to permeate us, putting us back together again.

_____

Thank You, Jesus, for making me whole through the infusion of Your life.

God is not a man, that he should lie,
nor a son of man, that he should
*   change his mind.*
Does he speak and then not act?
Does he promise and not fulfill?

Numbers 23:19 NIV

Most of us have little trust in people, especially men. They have abused us, used us, lied to us, given us empty promises, and proven themselves to be untrustworthy.

If we are going to be able to receive anything from God, we must first believe that He is not like the men we have known. God doesn't lie, and He doesn't change His mind.

God doesn't make promises He can't keep, and He won't make promises He has no intention of fulfilling. His word is true. What He says He will do, He does. God doesn't lie. God is not a man.

Dear God, I want to experience Your faithfulness. Help me trust You.

Behold, I send an Angel before you to keep you in the way and to bring you into the place which I have prepared.   Exodus 23:20

God promised to bring the people of Israel out of bondage and into an abundant land flowing with His blessings. He has prepared such a place for us as we journey out of our bondage and into wholeness.

We face the same choice the Israelites faced: to trust or not to trust. Their decision not to trust God resulted in their not entering the Promised Land. Instead, they died in the wilderness and their children enjoyed the fulfillment of God's promise.

Because of our wounding, we too are often unable to trust God or to embrace His promises. Let us overcome our patterns of unbelief and allow Him to guide us into the place of healing, where we can receive His abundance and blessing.

Thank You, Lord, for guiding me on this journey to wholeness, to the wonderful place You have prepared for me.

> *"For I will restore health to you*
> *And heal you of your wounds,"*
> *says the LORD.*
>
> Jeremiah 30:17

I am a survivor of child abuse and sexual molestation. I carry within me a hurting, wounded inner child. She's been the keeper of secrets that brought pain, and she's been the bearer of all my hidden shame. I've kept her hidden, afraid to let her out.

I am a survivor in recovery. God promises to restore my health—not just physically, but mentally and emotionally as well. He also promises to heal my childhood wounds. With Him I find the safety to reveal my wounded inner child and experience His comfort.

Father, thank You for providing safety for my inner child to be revealed and made whole as You heal the wounds of the past.

> *This is My commandment, that you love one*
> *another as I have loved you.*   John 15:12

For years my mother had waited for her special little girl. When I finally arrived, her disappointment was as great as her expectation had been. Instead of a petite little girl, she had an awkward, long-legged child with a disability. I felt the sting of her rejection. Virtually abandoned, I spent most of my time with an older brother, who cared for me but also abused me.

Not long ago in a moment of revelation, the Lord allowed me to feel the measure of pain my mother would feel for what she had caused me. In tears I released her, saying, "Father, forgive her for she did not know what she was doing."

The supernatural love of God is so great that He can bring about the miracle of love in us and help us forgive the very people who deeply wounded us.

Thank You, Lord, for Your love for me that transforms my heart, allowing me to love my mother.

*Beloved, do not avenge yourselves, but
rather give place to wrath; for it is
written, "Vengeance is Mine, I will repay,"
says the Lord.*   Romans 12:19

Many survivors of sexual abuse want to get back
at the people who hurt them so terribly. Wanting
revenge is a natural impulse, but it doesn't help anything.

Revenge may seem sweet, but it does not pro-
mote healing—it only feeds the pain and makes us
more like our abusers. After all, many of them were
victims themselves. They needed to forgive so they
wouldn't pass on the victimization. Now they need
our forgiveness, not revenge.

Remember, it is in forgiving that we are forgiven.

*Father, help me to forgive my abusers even when I don't feel
like it.*

And they shall repair the ruined cities,
The desolations of many generations.

Isaiah 61:4

I held my mother responsible and made her a silent partner to my offender. She should have known what was happening to me; she should have seen what he was doing. But when the same generational sin visited my family and my daughter was violated, I cried out, "How could this have happened?" I thought I had protected her, but my best efforts had failed.

My daughter's courageous decision to confront her abuser was the beginning of not just her healing but that of the generations before her and those that will follow. For as the Lord required me to forgive myself, I also forgave my mother and set her free from everything I had held against her.

Jesus came to repair ruined families and to deliver the generations from desolation. He will do it for each of us as we let go of our bitterness and humbly forgive.

Jesus, I forgive. Heal my family and free all the generations of my family.

He will rejoice over you with gladness.
Zephaniah 3:17

We watched her as our group prayed. She had named each perpetrator and asked God to remove their faces from His. As she spoke the last name her face softened, and quietly she walked to the chair that represented God. With silent tears she sat upon her Father's lap. For the first time in her life she knew His delight in her.

The goal of the enemy is to keep us from experiencing the love of our Father. He can do this by tempting us to see the faces of our abusers as God's face. If we peel away their faces and look into the Father's eyes, we will see His delight in us.

Father, give me the strength to see You as You really are and experience Your delight in me.

> *My soul shall make its boast in the LORD;*
> *The humble shall hear of it and be glad.*
>
> Psalm 34:2

Wrong ideas about God keep people from the joy of knowing Him as their Lord. We can be like open books to them, modeling what God is really like.

When we have experienced His love so deeply that we fall in love with Him, we cannot help but speak about Him. Our love shines when we tell of all He has done as He walks with us through good and bad times.

Those whose hearts are humbled to receive Him will be glad at the truth of our claims. Those who are not yet ready will at least be exposed to truth that challenges their beliefs.

Lord, may my boast of Your goodness gladden the hearts of the humble and challenge those who are not yet ready to receive.

Let your light so shine before men, that they may see your good works and glorify your Father in heaven.　　　Matthew 5:16

A prism disperses white light into its component colors. As the light enters through one of the prism's faces it is bent; upon leaving through another face it displays the full array of colors from red to violet.

The light that God shines through us should produce an array of good works. He tirelessly smooths and polishes the faces of our spiritual gifts so that each can reflect Him from a different angle. He desires that we position ourselves in such a way that our good works reflect His glory, not our own.

Lord, help me position myself in humility so that I may reflect Your glory through good works.

> *For the Lord hears your murmurings which you*
> *make against Him. And what are we? Your*
> *murmurings are not against us but against*
> *the LORD.*
> Exodus 16:8

I don't need this, Lord," I complained. Then I really got into grumbling about the person I was having to help, who neither liked me nor appreciated my efforts. "This is such a waste, Lord! I could be spending time with You." Surely the Lord would agree.

He did agree with one thing: my time *was* being wasted. However, I was the one who was wasting it. My grumbling was taking more time than if I had graciously met the person's needs. Worse, the Lord continued, my grumbling was really about Him, for He is in control of my life and was obviously allowing this "intrusion" for His purpose.

Griping about situations or people in our lives is really saying to God, "I'm unhappy about the way You're running my life."

Lord, help me to accept without grumbling whatever You put in my life and to seek Your purpose.

> *Let the words of my mouth and*
> *the meditation of my heart*
> *Be acceptable in Your sight,*
> *O LORD, my strength and my*
> *   redeemer.*   Psalm 19:14

During our recovery we often become totally self-absorbed. *My* abuse, *my* pain, *my* loss, *my* grief, *my* rage become the entire focus of *my* life.

We need to fix our minds on Jesus, who is our healer, deliverer, and restorer. We need to meditate on His Word because it is the truth. It is His Word that will comfort us in our affliction and give us life (see Ps. 119:50).

Scripture says we speak "out of the abundance of the heart" (Luke 6:45). By meditating on "whatever things are true . . . noble . . . just . . . pure . . . lovely [and] . . . of good report" (Phil. 4:8), we can be sure that the words we speak and the thoughts in our hearts will be acceptable in the Lord's sight.

Today, Lord, help me to fix my mind and heart on You and Your Word.

Be diligent to present yourself approved to God.
2 Timothy 2:15

There seemed to be a monster within me that always needed to be validated. The women's Bible study would satisfy the need for approval for an afternoon, but soon the void would recur. I constantly needed to be told I was okay, acceptable, worth something to someone.

Then I came to the period in my healing when God showed me that my insatiable need for approval was rooted in the humiliation of abuse. I surrendered my need to God. Daily I asked Him for the grace to lay it at His feet and to leave it there. Then, and only then, I found my approval in Him. My need was finally and forever satisfied.

Approval from others will always leave us needing more. Approval from the Lord always brings contentment and abundant life.

Just for today, Lord, I ask You to give me grace to seek only Your approval.

> *You shall not steal, nor deal falsely, nor lie to*
> *one another.*   Leviticus 19:11

Jesus knew all about the torture and abuse of my childhood, and He knew the reasons for my survival skills, dishonest as they were. Even in the midst of all my sin and dysfunction, I knew He loved me. I also knew that if I never did more than simply exist, He would still love me.

When I became an adult, mere existence was not enough. As I returned Jesus' love, I grew more and more dissatisfied with my life of lies. I determined to offer Him my all, no matter how shabby. For the first time in my life, I felt a hunger to live as He lives, to love as He loves, to experience passion and purpose in my heart. I wanted more.

Simply existing in our dysfunctional behavior is not living. Loving Jesus releases us, allowing us to live passionately, purposefully, and honestly.

O Lord, thank You for loving me in my falseness and inspiring me to live honestly.

> *For which of you, intending to build a tower,*
> *does not sit down first and count the cost.*
> Luke 14:28

Abused women can be very good at avoiding conflict. I had spent years keeping peace at any cost.

Now it seemed that God's goal of health and wholeness was costing me all that I had: my self-control, my self-respect, my pride, my fear of being honest. Every time I opened my mouth a conflict arose. All my dishonesty had to go; I couldn't pretend any longer. I was becoming honest and transparent for the first time in my life. I was scared.

The Lord allowed me to have those conflicts. It was the price I had to pay for healing. Allowing my true thoughts and feelings to flow was God's tool for healing my marriage.

Lord, forgive me for being so afraid of the cost of healing. Give me the courage today to pay the price.

He who follows righteousness and mercy
Finds life, righteousness and honor.

Proverbs 21:21

My daughter came home from school one day complaining that the other kids were calling her a "goody-goody." "Why?" I asked. "Because I get good grades and the teacher likes me." This made her feel very uncomfortable.

Strange how life affects each of us differently. I want to be a "goody-goody," to do and be only what is right. Ultimately we must each decide for ourselves. Do we do what is popular, following the crowd, or do we do what is right, finding God's promise of life, righteousness, and honor? As abused women we have often followed the crowd, wanting to please in order to avoid the pain.

Lord, help us to make wise decisions and follow after righteousness and mercy, no matter what the cost.

> *A person shall be put to death for his own sin.*
> Deuteronomy 24:16

As victims we fight a battle to keep the responsibility for what happened to us assigned to the right person. We must remember we are not responsible for the sins committed against us. God says each person will pay the penalty for his own sin. The perpetrator had free will and chose to do what he did.

Rationally, we would all agree that a child cannot be blamed for a sin committed against her. But perhaps we were not innocent little children. What if we were old enough to provoke or entice? Again, people are responsible for their own sins.

Repent of yours, but do not accept responsibility for the other person's sins. We were never *totally* to blame.

———————

Lord, I am willing to repent of my wrongdoing. Help me to distinguish between my sin and the sins committed against me.

*But I say to you that whoever looks at a woman
to lust for her has already committed adultery
with her in his heart.*   Matthew 5:28

Lust of the eye. "No big deal," we are told. "It's
only a *Playboy* magazine. It's classy. Look at those
wonderfully seductive pictures."

How many of us have felt terribly inadequate because we don't look like a centerfold? How many of
us have been victims of sexual abuse because of the
lust stirred within a man's heart and the actions that
followed?

God knows our weaknesses and vulnerability to
temptation. Jesus warns us that to lust with the eyes
is as wrong as the action of adultery. His words are a
warning for our protection.

*Father, help me to keep my eyes and mind on You and not look at
pornographic material. Help me to always value myself as Your
beautiful creation and not compare myself to others.*

> *Those from among you*
> *Shall build the old waste places;*
> *You shall raise up the foundations*
>   *of many generations;*
> *And you shall be called the Repairer*
>   *of the Breach,*
> *The Restorer of Streets to Dwell In.*
>   Isaiah 58:12

We who have been used, abused, and abandoned need to remember that Jesus Christ is the redeemer of all things. He will take our sins and the sins committed against us and He will transform us. The things we think disqualify us from His service are the very things He will use. He will use our experiences, our healing process, and our relationship with Him to minister life to others.

This is possible, because in Him we find the way to rebuild shattered lives on a new, solid foundation (Ps. 127:1). By His grace and indwelling Spirit we are empowered to touch others with His restoring love, bringing wholeness and reconciliation (Isa. 61:1–3; 2 Cor. 5:18).

Lord, today show me one way in which You want to use me as a restorer and rebuilder.

> *To everything there is a season,*
> *A time for every purpose under heaven.*
> Ecclesiastes 3:1

God has a time for everything. Often we get impatient with our progress or lack of it, when in fact we are right on schedule in God's time frame.

There are seasons in our lives just as there are seasons in nature. If our season is winter, God is doing deep inner work though little seems outwardly evident. A spring season finds us hopeful for new life, new beginnings. Summer brings days of fresh water and sunshine for our spirits. Autumn exposes us by revealing our true colors as we drop all our leafy coverings.

Our challenge is to discern the season and respond accordingly.

Lord, show me clearly my season and give me grace to learn its lessons.

> *Rest in the Lord, and wait patiently for Him.*
> Psalm 37:7

Resting and waiting may imply inactivity to some, but not when we wait on our Lord. Jesus desires each of us to develop patience, and we will have the opportunity to practice it often throughout our healing. We may prefer that God reveal everything at once so we can "get it over with," but God knows how much we can take at one time. Often He provides periods of rest, during which we must simply wait patiently on His perfect timing.

Even as we walk in wholeness, resting and waiting on the Lord will be the most important part of our day. When we rest in Him and wait on His counsel, He imparts wisdom to prepare us for the day. We become like those with whom we spend time. Let's spend our time with the Lord, who is love, joy, and peace.

Lord, give me the wisdom to rest daily in You, and, Lord, increase my patience as I wait for You.

Heal me, O Lord, and I shall be healed;
Save me, and I shall be saved, for You are my praise.
                                                    Jeremiah 17:14

There are days when I wake up mad. I find myself working hard not to explode at everyone around me. On the surface there is no apparent reason for the anger, but I have learned I can discover the root. It may be a dream I had during the night, reliving the abuse. Or it may be a situation that left me feeling like a victim. Perhaps it's fear or hurt coming to the surface that has not been fully resolved and needs further work. In any case, I know that I can trust God to reveal and heal. He is my praise.

Lord, I praise You for showing me the roots of my anger, and I receive Your healing and salvation from my past.

> *He leads me beside the still waters.*
> *He restores my soul.*
>
> Psalm 23:2–3

Change is painful, but God is always there to lead us through the pain. He allows us to see and understand only as much about ourselves and our situations as He knows we can handle. As we learn more about how He wants us to live, He slowly reveals to us the things in our lives that must change, such as memories of abuse and unhealthy relationships. Satan will give us a seemingly more desirable solution, one that is less painful and possibly even pleasurable, but God's ways are always the best. His ways restore our souls.

Lord, help me to remember that You are always there leading me and restoring me.

Bear one another's burdens.
Galatians 6:2

I had always been a loner. One of the hardest things to adjust to in my healing was the number of people God put in my life to help me along the way—counselors, friends, a large support group. I was overwhelmed. The Lord encouraged me to open my heart to them, to accept them, and to reach out and let them do the same, for they were there to fulfill His purpose.

As I did, I found each person was different. When things were difficult I knew which one to call, according to my need—the encourager, the exhorter, the comforter, the listener, the teacher. God had surrounded me with friends who embodied Him and provided love. They saw me through to health and wholeness.

Thank You, Lord, for the people You sent to be there for me. They helped bear my burdens as I walked through my healing.

MOMMY . . . WHERE WERE YOU?

Where were you
when I needed you?
I called. I cried.
I looked to see
if you would come,
if you would know
I needed you.

What should I have done?
I couldn't get away.
It hurt.
Then I was left,
to keep my secret all alone,
to cry and wonder,
"Where were you?"

I smiled
so you wouldn't ask, "Why
did you do wrong?"
I pretended
so you wouldn't know,
so you wouldn't go
and leave me sobbing.
"Mommy . . .
where were you?"

> *To everything there is a season,*
> *A time for every purpose*
> *under heaven. . . .*
> *A time to weep . . .*
> *A time to mourn.*
>
> Ecclesiastes 3:1, 4

Weeping and mourning are part of life. Sometimes they are not only allowable but necessary. When we suffer loss we must grieve in order to heal.

Because we are victims, we often fail to realize what we have lost because of our abuse. We have not recognized our losses, so we haven't mourned them.

There is a time to weep and a time to mourn. Just because we did not mourn our losses then does not mean it is too late to mourn them now. We are only now realizing our losses and feeling the pain. Now is the time to cry. Let the season of weeping and mourning begin. As we shed our cloaks of victimization and get in touch with our losses, we can begin to grieve.

Lord Jesus, be with me as I weep and mourn. Use this season to heal the pain of my losses.

> *Our fathers sinned and are no more,*
> *But we bear their iniquities.*
>
> Lamentations 5:7

Often we minimize our abuse. "It wasn't that bad," we say. "Worse things have happened to people." Or "It only happened once by a stranger—it isn't like it was incest. I'm fine; no big deal."

Then we see our children suffer the same kind of sexual sin perpetrated against us, and it takes on a new urgency. Our horror and anger at the violation of our children spur us to take the responsiblity to finally stop the pain of generations.

The attitudes and behavior of a victim are passed on through our families until one victim has the courage to break the silence of sexual abuse, bring it out in the open, and seek God's healing. Some of us do not find the courage until we see our children in the same situation.

Dear Jesus, give me the courage to take a stand, to break the pattern of victimization, and to put an end to the sins of the generations.

> *For my father and mother have*
> *forsaken me;*
> *But the Lord will take me up.*
> Psalm 27:10 NASV

One day I watched a little girl on a swing. She was cooing in delight as her daddy pushed her up high and the breeze tugged at her hair. There was a beautiful innocence about the scene, a serenity that God intended in their relationship.

When a father has robbed that innocence by sexually exploiting his child, it is devastating. We must remember that there is restoration ahead. We can reach out to our heavenly Father and allow Him to nurture us.

Healing is a process. First we grieve the loss of our earthly father's love. Next we allow God to establish a new foundation of pure love through His word, His Holy Spirit, and His people. Step by step, trust rebuilds and our innocence can be restored. It's a difficult process, but one that will result in great blessing.

Dear God, please step in where our earthly fathers have forsaken us.

*Assuredly, I say to you, unless you are converted
and become as little children, you will by no
means enter the kingdom of heaven.*

Matthew 18:3

How can I become like a child? Even when I was a child, I wasn't free to be a child. Fear, loneliness, and responsibility were handed to me at birth. The safest place for me was hiding in my closet, and sometimes even then my abusers would find me.

A child starts out in trust, without reservation. My little school friends did not worry. They could relax, be daring, and risk that swing or merry-go-round. But not I. Something awful would happen if I let down my guard for even a moment.

Become as a little child? That would surely bring pain. But somehow I could see Jesus on the other side of that pain and I couldn't resist. I began to cry and walk in His direction. Through my tears, I saw more clearly. I became a child and He became my Life.

Receive this little child into Your kingdom, Lord.

> *Behold, the LORD's hand*
> * is not shortened,*
> *That it cannot save;*
> *Nor His ear heavy,*
> *That it cannot hear.*
> *My God will hear me.*
> Isaiah 59:1; Micah 7:7

When I began having frightening memories of sexual abuse in my early childhood, a friend suggested I buy a stuffed animal. She thought it would be a comfort for the scared child within me.

As foolish as it sounded, I decided to try it and went shopping for just the right toy. After several minutes of intense scrutiny, I settled on a gray elephant. He could sit up and he scored high on squeezability, but it was his huge, pink, felt-lined ears that really drew me to him. Soon Al E. Phant, as he became known, was an important part of my healing process. Not only was it comforting to hold him, but his huge ears became a constant reminder to me that God always has ears big enough to hear.

Thank You, God, for always hearing me.

Yet regard the prayer of Your servant and [her] supplication, O Lord my God, and listen to the cry and the prayer which Your servant is praying before You today.   1 Kings 8:28

Lord, I want to thank You for being here for me again today. Some days, Lord, it gets so hard. It seems to take everything I've got just to make it through the day. Today was one of those days.

What a comfort it is to me to know that You do regard my prayers; You do listen to my cries. You listen today, and You will still listen tomorrow. Thanks, Lord, for healing me every day.

When I'm having a bad day the Lord says, "Child, for Me a thousand years is as one day. Whenever your prayer or cry comes to Me it is always today. I never sleep, so at every moment I am here for you. I love you and I will always regard your prayer and hear your cry."

Thanks, Lord. I love You, too.

Even to your old age, I am He,
And even to your gray hairs
I will carry you!

Isaiah 46:4

We will always be God's daughters. No matter how old we are, He still looks at us with a Father's love. In His mind, we are never too old to be called His children.

I guess that is why He ordained that I should re-live my traumatic childhood in midlife. To experience menopause while reliving child sexual abuse would not have been my choice. It was almost like He thought gray hair and a midlife crisis would enhance the healing process!

God says He will never forsake us, even when we're old and gray. He will never stop caring; He will never stop loving; He will never cease revealing those things that interfere with our relationship with Him. We will always be God's daughters, and He wants us healed and free.

Father, thank You for carrying me through the healing process.

The LORD your God, He is the One who
goes with you. He will not leave you nor
forsake you.
                              Deuteronomy 31:6

It is difficult for victims of abuse to reconcile God's
presence and power with the reality of rape, molestation, or incest. One night I saw it in the news
again—another child abused. I questioned, "Where
were You, Lord? How could You let this happen?"
His answer came with more anguish than I've ever
known. "I put My hand out for them to stop, to let
the children go. They would not. They pushed My
thoughts out and resisted My touch. My tears do not
stop as I grieve for My children."

My heart ached with a tiny portion of His grief.
Still, there was a wonderful peace that came with
the knowledge that He had not forsaken us. My
question shifted: "When will Your people listen,
Lord?"

Thank You, precious Lord, for always being with us. May we be
still enough to sense Your presence and quiet enough to hear
Your voice.

> *You will keep him in perfect peace,*
> *Whose mind is stayed on You,*
> *Because he trusts in You.*
>
> Isaiah 26:3

When we first realize that we have been a victim of sexual abuse we are shattered. Pain, confusion, shame, self-pity, anger—these and other emotions hit us.

If we stay in these emotions they will destroy us. But if we look to the Lord and lean on His promises, trusting Him, He will give us His perfect peace. Our lives may be overwhelmed with turmoil and the emotional pain of recovery, but He will fill us with His peace. He will give us an inner peace that leads to strength and hope.

Father, may I learn to trust You more each day and keep my mind on You, so that I might be filled with Your perfect peace.

> *And He said to me, "My grace is sufficient for you, for My strength is made perfect in weakness."*
> 2 Corinthians 12:9

For abused women each day presents its own challenges. There are days when we just don't have the strength to face them.

God has good news for us. We don't have to meet the challenges alone. In this verse, He tells us that His graciousness and unmerited favor will help us to withstand whatever comes against us. We need not fear because His power is complete. It thrives in our times of weakness.

Every morning we need only remember we can meet any challenge because His grace and His strength are ours.

Lord, I thank You that my weakness is an opportunity for Your grace and strength to be revealed.

> *You see the distress that we are in, how*
> *Jerusalem lies waste, and its gates are burned*
> *with fire. Come and let us build the wall of*
> *Jerusalem, that we may no longer be a*
> *reproach.*   Nehemiah 2:17

Nehemiah was a man of prayer and courage. He spent four months in prayer before he asked the king for the right to rebuild the walls of Jerusalem. The Jews had been home for nearly one hundred years but had rebuilt only the temple, leaving the walls of the city in shambles. Their powerful neighbors constantly were attacking them. Nehemiah surveyed the damage in the middle of the night so that he could make a plan to rebuild.

Being sexually abused causes such damage. Our gates are burned down and we are wasted. Remember that God can be your master planner. Let Him survey the damage, rebuild you, and protect you from attacks. _____

Help me to rebuild my life, O Lord.

Repent, and turn from all your transgressions,
so that iniquity will not be your ruin.
                                        Ezekiel 18:30

As a result of sexual abuse, we made decisions to live our lives in whatever way necessary to survive. Frequently those decisions increased our sorrows in later life.

Turning from a decision may or may not happen quickly. A sports car can make a very quick turn to go in the opposite direction on a narrow two-lane highway. However, an eighteen-wheeler may take quite a long time and may need six lanes of roadway to make the same kind of directional change.

We may take lots of time to change the direction of our lives, or change may come quickly with seemingly little effort. The good news is that if we continue on the highway of healing, eventually God will change the direction.

Lord, help me turn from the ways of ruin.

> *But put on the Lord Jesus Christ, and make no*
> *provision for the flesh, to fulfill its lusts.*
>
> Romans 13:14

One of the common problems of sexually abused women is fantasy. Early sexual exposure opens young minds to fantasize and escape from reality. If a father figure is the abuser or is not protective, the victim sometimes fantasizes finding a romantic male.

Although we were abused, we can choose to direct our thoughts to the Lord. Some suggest playing worship tapes, reading the Word, calling a friend, or journaling about healthy thoughts. It is a way of restructuring the old thinking processes.

Actively challenging our fantasies is one way of not making provision for the flesh.

Lord, fill me with thoughts of You and Your glory!

*Turn away from all your transgressions, so that
iniquity may not become a stumbling block to you.*
Ezekiel 18:30 NASV

Women who have been sexually abused often
have no idea how to have healthy intimate relationships. In the past sex was utilized to control and ma-
nipulate. It now becomes a stumbling block to
intimacy rather than a stepping stone.

One way to cast away wrong patterns is to prepare a list of all the males with whom you have had
ungodly relationships. Then get together with a
trusted friend, counselor, or pastor and pray over
each name. Ask God to forgive you as you also forgive and release them.

*Heavenly Father, give me the grace to admit my transgressions so
I can remove the stumbling blocks to You.*

> *Do not stir up nor awaken love*
> *Until it pleases.*
>
> Song of Solomon 2:7

This warning is uttered three times by Solomon. What is so important about it that it should be said three times?

When God created man and woman He gave each the ability to be sexually aroused and to respond. His purpose in doing so was twofold: to ensure procreation and to give each the ability to take pleasure in the other's body. However, being sexually awakened too early in life creates problems. This early stirring of desire can propel some into promiscuity. Others feel such guilt about sexual feelings that they judge them as bad and shut down sexually. Either path leads to problems.

We are fearfully and wonderfully made. God, who made us, knows how to repair the damage that was done. If we seek Him, He will bring us into balance.

Lord, I invite You to make the adjustments within me that will enable me to function sexually in the way You intended.

Become blameless and pure, children of God
without fault in a crooked and depraved
generation, in which you shine like stars.
Philippians 2:15 NIV

I remember looking at men and visualizing their genitals. I had not anticipated that thought; it just popped into my head. I shook my head, trying to get the picture to vanish. I thought I was really perverted, and I was sure men knew what I was thinking. I prayed fervently that God would help me with my dirty mind.

I finally got enough courage to seek help. As we prayed and sought the Lord, I discovered that my sexuality had been distorted by the molestations I had as a child. The molestations had involved pornography which led to perversion and lust. I prayed for God to cleanse my mind and spirit. Soon He cleansed me and robed me in His righteousness.

Dear Lord, purify my thoughts so I will shine like a star.

> *And they were both naked, the man and his*
> *wife, and were not ashamed.*   Genesis 2:25

God made man and woman to be pleasurable to each other. He intended the sexual union to be mutually fulfilling.

Unfortunately, for many of us sex has been less than God intended. We have been inhibited because we cannot be naked and not feel ashamed. We are ashamed of our own bodies, of how we look and function sexually. We are also uncomfortable with our husbands' bodies. We find it difficult to look, and we feel ashamed when they are aroused sexually.

We need to let God deal with our shame. He created us to be naked and not be ashamed. He can heal us and return to us the joy of God-given sexuality.

Lord, heal the places within me that give rise to my feelings of shame.

> *Put on the new self, which is being renewed in*
> *knowledge in the image of its Creator.*
>
> Colossians 3:10 NIV

Sexual molestation can cause difficulties for the intimacy of marriage. Certain touches, smells, or visual reminders may cause us to shut down or overreact.

I remember that when my husband began foreplay by fondling my breasts, I became stiff and unresponsive. When I remembered my cousin began molesting by fondling my breasts, I realized why I was shutting down with my husband.

It is not unusual for memories to be stimulated by similar touches, sounds, smells, or sights. God created us to be renewed; memories are a part of that renewal. Once we recall an unpleasant memory, the Lord is faithful to heal the painful images. As my memories were healed, I was able to enjoy intimacy with my husband. The Lord restored me, and I put on my new self!

Dear God, help me to put on a new self. Thank You for restoring me to the image of my Creator!

Blessings of the breasts and of the womb.
Genesis 49:25

Safe sex" is a common phrase now. The concept of safe sex takes on a new meaning for some sexual abuse victims. What God created for blessing, pleasure, and fulfillment became unenjoyable, unfulfilling, and for many of us, unsafe. We may experience flashbacks when touched, held, or spoken to in certain ways. Sometimes our flashbacks are triggered by the mere thought of having sex.

Sexual experiences become like minefields. With our mates we pick our way through as best we can, but inevitably there's an explosion. Only the Lord knows where the hidden explosives are, and He wants to defuse them, to sweep the area clean. If we are willing, He will turn the curse of sexual abuse into the blessings of God-given sexual intimacy.

Lord, I desire true sexual intimacy. Heal me sexually so I can experience the blessings of the breasts and womb.

Wash me, and I shall be whiter than snow.
Psalm 51:7

Bodily cleanliness is a two-sided issue with victims of sexual abuse. In an effort to end sexual abuse in adolescence, the frightened young girl may avoid baths, oral hygiene, or hair care. She may silently bear verbal abuse and harassment from people who want to change her behavior. It is easier, she reasons, to handle their dissatisfaction than to face the possibility of another sexual encounter.

After the perpetrator no longer has access she may then begin to take three or more showers or baths a day. This pattern represents her effort to wash away the filth of the violations; however, the external washing does not satisfy the need to feel clean within. Only Jesus' incredible love will wash us free of the feelings of filthiness. His words of love wash over us and we are made clean.

Jesus, wash away my feelings of filthiness.

> *As the deer pants for the water brooks,*
> *So pants my soul for You, O God.*
> *My soul thirsts for God, for the living God. . . .*
> *My soul longs, yes, even faints*
> *For the courts of the LORD;*
> *My heart and my flesh cry out for the living God.*
>   Psalm 42:1–2; Psalm 84:2

Are you stuck in your healing process? We all go through various stages as we heal. Because of shame and guilt many of us get stuck in a place where we have cut ourselves off from God. We pine away, feeling powerless to break free.

If that is the case, repent.

Jeremiah said: "I was ashamed, yes, even humiliated, because I bore the reproach of my youth" (Jer. 31:19). The solution was repentance, which opened the way for restoration and returning to God.

Once we long for Him, cry out for Him, and acknowledge that we cannot live without Him, then our healing begins in earnest.

I repent of hiding behind shame and guilt. Cleanse me, Lord, so our relationship can be restored.

The sheep follow him, for they know his voice.
John 10:4

Confusion is a terrible state in which to live. Most of us grew up trying to make sense out of the confusion in our lives. Through our healing we began to sort things out, and we found that we had good reason to be confused. Now I'm in my forties, and my first reaction to stress in family relationships is still confusion: What should I say? To whom can I turn?

Thank God, I have a Shepherd whose voice I know and who leads me into calm. Discerning His voice is a process, just like healing. We discover Jesus and receive Him into our hearts; we rebuild our lives on His foundation; we renew our minds by reading His Word; we give Him opportunity to speak by being quiet and listening to Him. He will speak; we will recognize His voice and gladly follow where He leads.

Thank You, my Shepherd, for speaking to me so that I may know Your voice and follow.

> *I am the Lord . . .*
> *Who teaches you to profit,*
> *Who leads you by the way*
>   *you should go.*
>   Isaiah 48:17

I grew to love the Lord as He healed me. I also experienced a tremendous hunger to know all about Him, learning from gifted teachers, preachers, and books.

Praying one morning, I saw a room with two tables. One was filled with TV programs, tapes, and books. The Lord said, "This table is good and acceptable for a time. But, child, I want you to come to the other table."

I looked and saw that it was empty. "But, Lord," I protested, "there is nothing on it." "Yes, it is not what you want," He agreed, "but it is what you need. Come aside for a season and draw from My well. I will lead you and you will profit from My teaching."

Let us allow the Lord to be our primary teacher, both in healing and in health.

Lord, thank You for letting me draw from Your well.

For My yoke is easy and My burden is light.
Matthew 11:30

The car ahead was struggling to keep up with the flow of traffic. Strapped to its top was a baggage carrier. The carrier added three feet to the height of the car and hindered the car's aerodynamics. The added height created a wall of resistance against the air. Even with the accelerator pushed to the floor the car could not keep up, and the other cars passed it by.

The baggage of past sexual wounds and offenses can hinder our progress in the Lord. He has designed us in a spiritually aerodynamic way to push through the winds of life. If we detach the baggage of our abuse, we can stay in His flow.

Lord, help me to unload my baggage and take on Your yoke and burden.

> *Cease from anger, and forsake wrath.*
> Psalm 37:8

Do you remember the bitterness, anger, and rage you felt and may still be feeling toward the person or persons who abused you? These emotions are a natural reaction. We want to lash out and hurt the people who have hurt us. We want to make them suffer as we have suffered.

As we look to Christ for our healing and allow His love to permeate us, a miraculous thing happens. He begins to change these emotions and replace them with His love and acceptance. He does not just hide these feelings from us; He actually removes them from us.

Allow Him to do this. Release your anger. Release your bitterness. Release your rage to your heavenly Father.

———————

Father, remove my bitterness, anger, and rage and fill me with Your love.

> *"Lord, how often shall my brother sin against me, and I forgive him? Up to seven times?"*
> *Jesus said to him, "I do not say to you, up to seven times, but up to seventy times seven."*
> Matthew 18:21–22

How often are we like Peter? We want the Lord to draw a line for us separating what we must forgive and what we don't have to forgive. He has.

The number seven is the number of completion. Jesus' instruction to forgive "seventy times seven" indicated a number too large to calculate. He meant we are to forgive infinitely. Forgiveness is a decision of the will and a process in our hearts. We are to keep forgiving until the forgiving process is a completed work in our hearts, no matter how many times we are sinned against.

Lord, I choose to forgive those who have sinned against me. Help me continue the process of forgiveness in my heart.

> *Therefore He is also able to save to the uttermost those who come to God through Him, since He ever lives to make intercession for them.*
>
> Hebrews 7:25

I shuddered when I read this Scripture. I instantly knew the Lord was telling me that abusers are not beyond His saving power. His heart is turned toward them because He is not willing for anyone to perish. He desires that all should come to repentance (2 Peter 3:9).

Jesus is in constant intercession on behalf of abusers. He prays they will experience the grace of God through the convicting power of His Spirit. He prays that they will be delivered from the bondage of sin. If that is God's desire for our abusers, how can we wish for them to be damned? The Lord Himself taught us to pray: "Forgive us our sins, for we also forgive everyone who sins against us" (Luke 11:4 NIV).

———————

Lord, I repent of my desire to punish those who have abused me.

And he prayed that he might die.
1 Kings 19:4

The great prophet Elijah prayed to die as he was fleeing from Jezebel. In utter despair he hid in a cave. The angel of the Lord appeared to him, instructing him to leave the cave and stand in the presence of the Lord.

When Elijah peered out he saw a powerful display of wind, earthquake, and fire, but the Lord was not in them. In the total silence that followed, Elijah heard "a still small voice." He went to the mouth of the cave, and there the Lord spoke encouragingly to him.

Sometimes in our despair we, too, pray to die. In those times we need to leave our hiding place and dare to stand in the stillness of the Lord's presence. He will speak words of encouragement to us, just as He did to Elijah.

I shall not die, but live,
And declare the works
of the LORD
(Ps. 118:17)

> *His countenance was like the sun shining
> in its strength.*
> Revelation 1:16

Looks can be deceiving in the presence of fog. Driving or walking in fog distorts our vision. It makes the road or pathway appear to be uphill even when it is level. It is not until the sun shines upon the land that the fog is burned off and visibility returns.

The depression that stems from sexual abuse can keep us walking around in an emotional fog. Even the simplest requirements of life seem to be an uphill battle. This depressive fog can be just as deadly as an atmospheric fog that results in auto accidents.

Allowing God to shine upon our heart will burn off that depressive fog. We can look in His face and see all the warmth we have ever longed to enjoy.

Lord, allow me to see Your face. Then the depression will no longer distort my vision.

*Whether it was two days, a month, or a year
that the cloud remained above the tabernacle,
the children of Israel would remain encamped
and not journey; but when it was taken up, they
would journey.*
Numbers 9:22

God placed a cloud over the tabernacle so His children would know that He was with them. The Israelites followed the cloud when it moved and stopped when the cloud stopped. Today, through Jesus Christ, God has sent His Holy Spirit to be our guide.

Leaving my childhood home I felt like I was in a cloud, rather than being led by one. Incest left me in a fog. Recovery has been like lifting the fog. I have sorted through it all with the Holy Spirit as my guide. The journey is often difficult and painful, but God always lets me know that He is with me. Whether it lasts two days, a month, or a year, He will never leave me.

Holy Spirit, guide me on this journey.

> *A time to weep,*
> *And a time to laugh;*
> *A time to mourn,*
> *And a time to dance.*
> Ecclesiastes 3:4

As we journey down the long road of recovery, we will weep for and mourn many losses. There will not be a single season of grieving but many scattered times. In between the times of tears and pain, God wants us to experience times of joy.

"A merry heart does good, like medicine" (Prov. 17:22). What better medicine is there than laughing and playing? There is a time to dance, to jump for joy.

"Weeping may endure for a night, but joy comes in the morning" (Ps. 30:5). Even if we have no other reasons to laugh and jump for joy, being released from the pain of grieving should be enough.

We need to take time to do things that will make us laugh. Get out among people in places where they are having a good time. Enjoy this season while it lasts!

Thank You, Lord, for turning my mourning into dancing.

WANTED . . . FOUND

When I was a child, I wanted
to be held,
to trust the arms around me
and not get hurt,
to have no monster with a scary face
come and stare at me . . .

To have someone's neck
to press into and hide my face,
to not hear the screams inside my head
which told me I was bad, only bad.

Instead,
a pillow was my friend. It cradled
the voice which barbed my dreams
each silent, sorry night . . .

Until the day,
this present day,
in which I've found
a place to rest
within my own soul
and an orphan's home
in God's warm embrace.

> *But Jesus said, "Let the little children come to*
> *Me, and do not forbid them."*

Matthew 19:14

Abused as a small child, I needed but never received Jesus' comfort. When I was five, my daddy left. Nobody ever told me that God is a father who never leaves you. My youth was robbed by more abuse, and still no one told me that Jesus was there for me.

When I became an adult the pattern of abuse continued, until finally someone told me about Jesus. As He softened my heart, I realized that I needed healing for my childhood wounds. I became as a child again. With each painful memory I came to Jesus. He lovingly touched each childhood pain and brought healing to that part of my life.

Thank You, Lord, that we are never too old to become like children in Your presence. Thank You for healing the pain of my childhood.

> *Then Jesus said, "Father, forgive them, for they
> do not know what they do."*   Luke 23:34

A sexually abused child often grows up emotionally isolated. Her siblings may actually envy her for the extra attention she seems to receive; they are often unaware of the abuse that goes with the attention. This was the case in my home. As much as I strived for my sisters' approval, I continued to be rejected. Eventually resentment grew within me and I hardened my heart against them.

My bitterness against women and my resulting isolation continued into adulthood. Even when I became a Christian and the Lord brought me all new sisters, I still had such a problem that I almost stopped attending the women's Bible studies. In my loneliness I cried out to the Lord, and He showed me the cause of my problem. I had made judgments against all women when I refused to forgive my sisters. But when I forgave them for rejecting me, the judgments stopped and friendship flowed.

Unforgiveness binds us; forgiveness sets us free.

Teach me, Jesus, to forgive those who reject me.

For You have formed my inward parts;
You have [knit] me in my mother's womb.

Psalm 139:13

God knows us and has known us since before we were born. He is aware of our characters and personalities, our gifts and talents, our pains and our joys. He has a use for each of us in His kingdom, but first we must desire above all things a relationship with Him. We must surrender all that we are, have been, and will be to Him.

When we give ourselves to God and open our wounded inward parts to Him, He heals, molds, and shapes us for His purposes. Only He, who knows all things, is able to use the painful parts of our lives, knitting them into something strong and beautiful. He is waiting for us to invite Him in.

Father, You who knew me before I was born, help me to make myself fully known to You and to surrender myself completely.

> *I will instruct you and teach you*
> *in the way you should go;*
> *I will guide you with My eye.*
> Psalm 32:8

Isn't God good to provide us with a supernatural Counselor to continually teach us and guide us in the ways of the Lord?

No longer do we need to wait on edge for our next therapy appointments. No more do we find ourselves white-knuckled between sessions. As Christians, we have within us the very Counselor whose wisdom all Christian counselors seek! And He is with us forever, every moment, day or night. We can turn our problems over to Him and await His perfect counsel.

As we learn to get in touch with the Holy Spirit, our Counselor within, we need less counsel and care from others. God has truly thought of everything to ensure our healing and wholeness.

Thank You, Holy Spirit, for being my constant Companion and Counselor to guide me in the way I should go.

> *For I know that in me (that is, in my flesh)*
> *nothing good dwells.* Romans 7:18

It's frequently said that healing comes about only as we begin to value ourselves. Our negative self-images must be replaced by positive convictions of our self-worth. Where then does "dying to self" come in? We hear it taught but it sounds foolish— the very opposite of what we've learned in recovery.

Actually it's our flesh, or worldly self, that controls us and needs to die. If Jesus is really Lord of our lives, then we will actively surrender our fleshly desires to His control. We choose to put to death, or deny, those ungodly desires within us that have only compounded our misery. We must think enough of ourselves, our total persons, to lay aside our controlling desires and allow God to bless us.

Thank You for teaching me through Your kindness, Lord, that Your desires for me are far better than any fleshly desire that dwells in me.

But then I shall know just as I also am known.
1 Corinthians 13:12

Which is more wonderful, to know or to be known?

We often race headlong, thirstily seeking more knowledge about ourselves and our abuse. But a deeper, more abiding joy can emerge. The joy of being known by Him. Sometimes the pain of loneliness becomes overpowering. There seems to be no other human soul who can fully understand our hurts, aspirations, secret desires, fears, and insecurities.

There is only one answer to our loneliness: we are fully known by God. He knows, understands, and cares. What a priceless, incomprehensible treasure!

Oh, Father, help me to rest in the assurance that You know me—every delightful and terrible thing about me—and love me still.

But it is good for me to draw near to God;
I have put my trust in the Lord God,
That I may declare all Your works.

Psalm 73:28

Drawing near to God is not a luxury; it is necessary for our healing. At first it was difficult to allow myself time alone with God. It seemed foreign to me, self-indulgent to take time out for just God and me.

But God is not self-indulgent, and His healing is not just for self. He wants us to be living testimonies of His love. When we are whole our very lives declare Him.

Our healing must be a priority before we can reflect His works. God heals what He reveals, but revelation will not come unless we make time to draw near to Him.

Lord, help me draw near to You without feeling guilty for our time together or the time it takes to be healed.

For God has not given us a spirit of fear, but of power and of love and of a sound mind.

2 Timothy 1:7

I was awakened by the sound of my pounding heart. What did I have to fear? I was safe, sitting next to my husband on the plane; yet I felt trapped with no way of escape. I had felt these feelings before—once in the back seat of a car with friends. Again, it was a seemingly safe place, and yet I felt great fear.

Oh, how the memories of the past can bind us with fear in the present. Yet in the Bible God says 365 times, "fear not." He knew we would need at least one "fear not" each day. As I cry out daily to the Lord to deliver me from my fear, He hears me, heals my past, and gives me a sound mind.

Lord, reveal and heal the hidden areas of my past which bind me with fear in the present.

> *Then Jesus said to the twelve, "Do you also*
> *want to go away?" Then Simon Peter answered*
> *Him, "Lord, to whom shall we go? You have the*
> *words of eternal life."*
>   John 6:67–68

For almost twenty years I ignored and denied the headaches, except for periods when nothing would help but a trip to the emergency room. There seemed to be no physical reason for my pain, and I gave up on physicians being able to help me. But when the over-the-counter pain medication I was addicted to was suddenly removed from the market, I could no longer ignore the pain.

I had accepted the lie that there were no reasons for the pain. Just as the disciples of Jesus said, "We have no place to go," neither did I. Desperately I asked the Lord to deal with my heart, and He began to unravel the emotional pain of my past. I discovered that the pain was not an enemy, but a blessing. It was the tool Jesus used to begin my journey of healing and discovery of who I am in Him.

Dear Lord, thank You for having the words that gave me life.

> *"For I know the thoughts that I think toward*
> *you," says the LORD, "thoughts of peace and not*
> *of evil, to give you a future and a hope."*
>   Jeremiah 29:11

M̲y sexual abuse had gone totally undetected. For years I seemed normal and unaffected until the day I was physically assaulted. That trauma made all the hidden memories surface.

I became angry with God for allowing what I had so painstakingly hidden to come crashing back into my consciousness.

The Lord knew that until I faced the hidden issues, I would never be free to be the person He created me to be. Although I had repressed them, the memories affected every aspect of my life. My only hope for a peaceful future was to face the pain of the past.

———————

Lord, today I totally surrender myself to You. Uncover whatever is necessary to bring about Your plans of peace and a future for me. Help me face my wounds so I can be the person You have created me to be.

> *They looked to Him and were radiant,*
> *And their faces were not ashamed.*
>
> Psalm 34:5

A sore that is covered up and not exposed to the light will fester, become infected, and send its poison throughout the body. If we think that the sexual abuse we suffered is a secret that we dare not share, then it becomes like a hidden sore. As long as we hide our past in the darkness, we allow Satan, our enemy, to hold it over us. Our pain and shame fester and infect every part of our lives.

Let us be courageous and expose our secrets to the light of Jesus. He will not condemn us. He will gently remove our shame and fully redeem us. Our darkness will be transformed and our joy will be apparent to all, for our faces will shine with His radiance.

Lord, thank You that when I look at You, I look different.

> *The LORD is near to those who have a*
> *broken heart,*
> *And saves such as have a contrite spirit.*
>
> Psalm 34:18

Victims of abuse hide their pain until they can finally admit their broken hearts, face their pasts, and work through their issues honestly. In the meantime their lives are usually out of control in the area in which the pain is manifested.

It's hard to take ownership for sins that are rooted in someone else's sin against us. Jesus knows the roots of our sin just as He knows the cause of our broken hearts, and He wants to save us from both.

We must take ownership of our behavior and come to Him with a contrite spirit. Then we can experience the wonder of His healing balm as it pours over and through us, cleansing our sins and making our hearts whole once more.

Dear Lord, I confess my sin to You. Mend my broken heart and honor my contrite spirit by forgiving my sins.

> *Bless the LORD, O my soul,*
> *And forget not all His benefits. . . .*
> *Who redeems your life from*
> *destruction.*   Psalm 103:2, 4

Penis . . . pain. For many survivors of sexual abuse, the words are interchangeable. This is especially true for those who are introduced to abuse at a young age. A man's penis was a weapon of torment and destruction. It ripped flesh and bruised deep within. Its size could make a little girl gag and choke.

This was never Jesus' plan. He meant for the male and female sexual organs to be a source of joy, comfort, and fulfillment between two married adults. That can seem impossible to those who have suffered sexual abuse. Just remember that Jesus has the power to cleanse our destructive sexual memories and replace them with His perspective. If it would take a miracle, that is His specialty.

Jesus, redeem me from the destructive memories of my sexual past.

*Therefore know that the LORD your God, He is
God, the faithful God who keeps covenant and
mercy . . . with those who love Him and keep
His commandments.*   Deuteronomy 7:9

God prompted me to go back through my journal
and write out His promises to me. I discovered a
vital truth: God is still a God of covenant. His promises still take the form of a pact, which means that
two enter into agreement.

He asks us to do our part and He vows, in turn, to
do His. Sometimes our part is simply to trust, but
other times we have a more active role. For example, God promises to use our changed lives to help
other women recover, but only if we do what He
asks and go where He sends us.

The fulfillment of His promises are based on our
responses to the covenant. Let us always answer,
"Yes."

Lord, I say yes to Your promises and commands for my life.

> *My beloved is mine, and I am his.*
> Song of Solomon 2:16

God's plan for sex in marriage is a oneness of body, spirit, and mind. Sex should be the closest, most intimate relationship possible between a man and a woman.

When the intimacy and spiritual oneness are taken out, only the physical act of sex remains. As abused women we may have known this detached, mechanical sex. Perhaps we have known only feelings of pleasure, but none of intimacy.

There is more. God's creative plan embraces spirit, mind, and body—a total oneness. Ideal sex means a total commitment and sharing of self with another human being. In this intimacy is true sexual fulfillment.

Father, help me to know a relationship of complete oneness with my beloved. Break down the barriers that are keeping us from having such a total intimacy.

> *I will say of the LORD, "He is my*
> *refuge and my fortress;*
> *My God, in Him I will trust."*
> Psalm 91:2

 M y first venture from the "nest" threatened to be a disaster. I flew bravely, only to crash into a wall. I was tempted to limp back to the nest, vowing never to try again.

It was a week-long writing seminar with fifty strangers, the first time I'd done anything alone. The instructor's harsh critique sent me flying to my refuge. God assured me this was His will, and I trusted Him. Incredibly, I was at peace despite the criticism. I was able to detach, recognizing that my self had not been rejected, and receive the truth. I remained open and available to the other women who later wanted to talk.

God turned a potential disaster into healing.

Thank You, Lord, that You are my refuge and fortress in whom I can trust at all times.

> *Now to Him who is able to do exceedingly*
> *abundantly above all that we ask or think,*
> *according to the power that works in us.*
>
> Ephesians 3:20

I spoke to a friend today about seeking healing of the emotional wounds caused by sexual abuse in her childhood. "I'm okay," she assured me. "It doesn't bother me anymore. I don't even think about it."

It's easy to assume that since the abuse isn't consciously in our thoughts, we don't need healing. But the truth is that until the Lord heals the emotional wounds caused by abuse, our lives are deeply affected.

When we allow God to open our eyes, we will see how the abuse has influenced us, especially in our intimate relationships. The role we play—whether victim or controller or even avoider—is a product of the abuse.

Let us not turn away from God's healing power, content with where we are. Let us welcome Him to work within us all that He is able to do!

Thank You, Lord, that Your desires for me are more than I can even imagine.

For your Maker is your husband,
The Lord of hosts is His name.
Isaiah 54:5

Our Lord desires to be our husband and have a most intimate relationship with us. This intimacy will not only fill us and furnish our every need, but it will also demonstrate God's original plan for human relationships. Abuse has damaged our willingness and ability to be intimate.

Intimacy requires risk. We have to risk conflict, misunderstandings, and rejection. It also takes time. We need to spend time with God in Scripture, prayer, and just listening to Him.

How are we responding? Are we seeking an intimate relationship with Him? If we are, our Maker will become our husband.

Lord, help me to respond to You as my husband. Help me to learn intimacy by establishing an intimate relationship with You.

*Your love, O LORD, reaches to
  the heavens,
Your faithfulness to the skies.
Your righteousness is like
  the mighty mountains,
Your justice like the great deep.*
Psalm 36:5–7 NIV

What marvelous words. His love reaches to the heavens and His faithfulness to the skies! Have you ever doubted God's love or faithfulness?

Recently I sat on a beach along the Pacific Coast, feeling the cool spray of salt water, filling my lungs with the fresh, clean air. I filled my senses with the presence of God. His mighty mountains were at my back; a warm sun and infinite blue sky covered my head. Most magnificent of all was the constant rolling, crashing power of the ocean's waves. It reminded me of Him.

We never question this constancy of mountains, ocean, sun, or sky. In this very tangible way our God is telling us that He will never fail us.

Thank You, Father, for Your unfailing love. Help me to sense Your presence in everything that touches my life.

*For God so loved the world that He gave His
only begotten Son, that whoever believes in Him
should not perish, but have everlasting life.*

John 3:16

Today my friend said, "God is love. He loves you
and wants you to live with Him forever."

"She doesn't mean this!" I thought. Why would
she tell me such lies? Who would love me? I'm a
person full of scars and pain—pain that changed the
very course of my life. Why would God want me?

My friend's patience eventually won out. With
each tiny timid step, she gradually led me to the
Lord. There I found the courage to open the long-
closed inner doors of my heart and mind.

Jesus is waiting to take our sorrows, pain, and unworthiness. When we open our hearts to Him, we
begin to know love.

Thank You, Lord, for loving me so much.

> *I, the LORD, search the heart,*
> *I test the mind,*
> *Even to give every man according*
> *to his ways,*
> *And according to the fruit of his*
> *doings.*   Jeremiah 17:10

Mainframe computer databases hold vast amounts of data. If information is needed about a particular subject, the computer will search for qualifying data. Decisions are then made based on that data.

Our brains work in a similar way. They have stored every experience we have ever had, along with the smells, sounds, and feelings that accompany the incident. Throughout the day our brains search their data to access the information we have stored about situations similar to the current one. Then they react the way they did in similar situations in the past.

To change we must allow the Holy Spirit to override our reactive thinking and take time to respond in the way the Lord wants.

Search my mind, Lord, and change the way I think.

*Therefore judge nothing before the time, until
the Lord comes, who will . . . bring to light the
hidden things of darkness.* 1 Corinthians 4:5

Oh, you just have a low tolerance for pain." I've
heard those words again and again from my husband. I used to get so angry. The pain was still there,
but somehow that statement seemed to deny it.

One day in prayer, a picture flashed before my
eyes. I saw myself as a child crossing the street on a
snowy day. From out of nowhere, a taxicab hit me. I
remember the pain, but fear made me think that no
one should know what happened. I pushed the pain
away and ran home.

I realized I had learned to deny my own pain because I had been victimized. It appeared as though I
had a low tolerance for pain, but in fact I had hidden
the pain for so long that it became uncontrollable. It
took God to bring to light the hidden truth.

How much pain have you hidden because of
those who victimized you?

*Lord, You reveal to heal. Let Your grace be sufficient for me to
face my pain and be healed.*

Be angry, and do not sin.
Psalm 4:4

Anger is a God-given emotion. Scripture reveals that God Himself gets angry. Jesus was angry when He cleared the temple.

It is all right to be angry. The challenge is to learn how to experience anger without sinning in the process—against ourselves through suppression or repression or against others with wrongful expressions.

Channeling our anger creatively can help. Writing letters and then burning them can be a way of releasing deep anger. Throwing ice or going to a batting cage can physically release pent-up anger. Having a water pistol fight or a pillow fight can be fun while relieving angry energy.

God does not want us to "stuff" our anger. He wants us to express it in ways that are not harmful to ourselves or others.

Today, Lord, help me feel my anger and deal with it constructively.

I, the LORD, search the heart.
Jeremiah 17:10

Scripture tells us we do not know what is in our own hearts. This is especially true when we have been deeply wounded. The pain numbs our feelings and hinders our abilities to discern our own hearts.

Whenever I need to get in touch with the condition of my heart, I become like a child again. With paper and crayons in hand, I ask the Lord to search my heart. As I sit quietly before Him I begin to draw a picture of the heart He shows me.

Once I've drawn it I present it to Jesus. No matter how ugly or broken it looks, I give it to Him. Then I pray for Him to heal my heart, and as He does, He gives me visions of a new heart. As I draw the new heart, I receive His healing love.

Thank You, Lord, for searching my heart and healing its wounds.

Make us glad according to the days in which
You have afflicted us,
And the years in which we have seen evil.
Psalm 90:15

Some say that Moses wrote this psalm after wandering in the desert for forty years. Because of the disobedience and strong will of the children of Israel, God led them on a path of humility. Moses appealed to the Most High to return quickly and restore their gladness.

Do you feel like Moses, who saw evil and had nothing to be glad about? Have you been wandering in the desert for a long time? Throughout this psalm and others you will see God's compassion and mercy. Go to Him. Ask Him, just as Moses did, to make you glad. Tell Him of your troubles and the evil you have seen. He is waiting for you to stop wandering. His arms are open wide to you.

Lord, make me glad.

Therefore by the deeds of the law no flesh will be justified in His sight, for by the law is the knowledge of sin.   Romans 3:20

The goal of auto emissions testing is to provide clean air for ourselves and future generations. Few would deny the worthiness of this goal. However, most of us merely want to pass the required standard and would never think of going beyond it to make the air even cleaner.

God desires us to have clean hearts for the benefit of ourselves and future generations. We must not try only to meet the minimum requirement of His laws. We must work to reach His goal of being like Him.

Create in me a clean heart, O God.

But if you do not forgive men their trespasses,
neither will your Father forgive your trespasses.
Matthew 6:15

It is difficult to forgive the people who have hurt you even though God is clear throughout His Word that He brings justice.

One of the ways I found the resolve to forgive was to separate the sin from the sinner. I wrote a letter to the sin I hated and burned it as an offering of a sweet fragrance to the Lord. As for the sinner, I realized he must have been in bondage himself. I also found that hanging on to the unforgiveness was keeping me a victim by not allowing me the freedom to go to my Father on behalf of my own transgressions. I forgave and allowed the Lord to deal with my abuser.

Dear Lord, help me realize how dear Your forgiveness is and what price we pay when we choose not to forgive our transgressors.

A house divided against itself will fall.
Luke 11:17 NIV

One of the first realizations many women in recovery have is that each of us is "a house divided." Unconsciously, we have divided ourselves, putting different traumas and emotions in separate compartments. It is a survival technique that works well until the memories and feelings come spilling out. Then we begin to fall apart.

God wants us to allow those compartment walls to come tumbling down. That means we have to be willing to remember and to feel again. We have to accept ourselves as weak, vulnerable, and wounded. Most of all, we need to bring the pieces of our lives to the only One who can piece them back together.

My Creator, Jesus, is the only One who can make my divided house whole again.

Lord, reveal where my house is divided and give me the grace to cooperate with Your rebuilding process.

> *The Father of mercies and God of all comfort,*
> *who comforts us in all our tribulation, that we*
> *may be able to comfort those who are in any*
> *trouble, with the comfort with which we*
> *ourselves are comforted by God.*
>
> 2 Corinthians 1:3–4

The greatest gifts we can offer other women are understanding and comfort. Because nothing God allows is ever wasted, we know with certainty that He will not waste the pain, fear, and shame we experienced in our abuse.

Just as God comforted us when we cried out to Him, so also we are to comfort those around us who are in abusive situations. We have been through the fire. We can identify with them. We can pass on to them the comfort and love God gave to us.

Thank You, Father, for Your comfort in my pain. Give me opportunities to share Your comfort with others.

LORD, my heart is not haughty,
Nor my eyes lofty.
Neither do I concern myself with great
matters,
Nor with things too profound for me.
Surely I have calmed and quieted my
soul,
Like a weaned child with his mother;
Like a weaned child is my soul
within me.   Psalm 131:1–2

The question why? can ruthlessly haunt victims of sexual abuse. Sometimes it is so oppressive it becomes too heavy to bear! The pain takes on a life of its own, ready to engulf and enslave us.

Answering the unanswerable is a challenge God is fully capable of doing. Our part is to ask the questions bravely, wait in quietness, and accept whatever His answer may be.

Oh, Lord, quiet my soul before You, so that I may hear Your voice and accept Your answer.

FACES OF FEAR

When I was a child
small things frightened me:
measured footsteps on the stairs,
a certain smile,
words that rolled through lips
and lingered in the air,
a door opened slowly
late at night.
Wide-eyed, silent,
frozen with fear,
part of me would disappear
as if I'd vanished in the night.

Now the fear I face is this:
Where am I? . . .
and who . . . ?

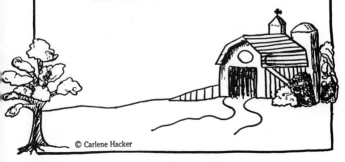

© Carlene Hacker

> *Say to those who are fearful-hearted,*
> *"Be strong, do not fear!"*
>
> Isaiah 35:4

One of the biggest hindrances to our recovery is fear. Perhaps that is why there are 365 passages on fear in the Bible—one for each day of the year! We fear the past because the enemy constantly uses it to remind us of our failures. We fear the future because we don't know what it will bring.

We must constantly be reminded to be strong and fearless. God's Word assures us that, aside from a healthy fear of Him, there is nothing else to fear. As His children, we are even guaranteed that God will turn to good those things in our lives that Satan meant to use to harm us.

Let us take hold of the confidence that we have in the Lord. In His strength we can deal with the past and face the future without fear.

Thank You, Lord, for strengthening my fearful heart.

For God has not given us a spirit of fear; but
of power and of love and of a sound mind.
2 Timothy 1:7

My problems with fear and denial come in waves. I often think, "I must have made that up. What if I'm wrong? He wouldn't have hurt me like that." But I'm not crazy. I didn't make up any of this stuff! I know what I know. When the next spasm of doubt hits, I need to remind myself of where it comes from.

Since God has not given me the spirit of fear, I know who it comes from. Since it has to be given, I can refuse to receive it. I don't choose to live in fear and doubt!

I try to flood my mind with the truth that God loves me and that I am of value to Him. In that way I am better able to face the enemy who makes me feel fearful and crazy.

Father, remind me in the fearful times that the doubt and confusion are not from You.

> *Your life is hidden with Christ in God.*
> Colossians 3:3

For victims of abuse, safety is a paramount issue. We must feel safe in order to escape the nightmare and begin the recovery process.

Scripture assures us that because we have accepted Jesus, we are now covered by Him and hidden in God. He is our hiding place (see Ps. 32:7). We can trust in the shelter of His wings (see Ps. 61:4). He will cover us with His feathers, and the shadow of His wings will provide a refuge until the calamities have passed (see Pss. 91:4; 57:1). Because we dwell in His secret place, when we go to bed at night we can sleep peacefully (see Pss. 91:1; 4:8). He who keeps us will neither slumber nor sleep. He will preserve us from all evil (see Ps. 121:4, 7).

We can rejoice in the shadow of His wings (see Ps. 63:7). There is no God like our God, the eternal God. He is indeed our refuge, our hiding place. Underneath us are His everlasting arms (see Deut. 33:26–27).

Thank You, Lord, that because of Jesus I am hidden in You. Thank You for being my place of safety.

My grace is sufficient for you, for My strength is made perfect in weakness.

2 Corinthians 12:9

Weakness: lacking in strength or stability; ineffectual. That is how the world views us as we yield our lives and wills to God. But when we compare our strength with God's strength, we know we are limited and He is limitless. We are erratic, but He is unchanging.

It would be foolish for us not to trust in God for help and guidance. When we cry out in despair from the effects of years of abuse, He is there. His strength fills us as we yield to Him. We must allow His strength to become perfect in our weakness.

Lord, I yield my will to You so that I might receive Your grace and strength.

I am like a broken vessel.
Psalm 31:12

I feel so broken. I just feel *so broken.*"

Those were the only words I could say as I cried. It was true; I was broken. My life had been badly scarred by abuse and pain.

We all may experience that deep sense of brokenness periodically during our healing process. During those times we have this consolation: God is a master potter who can repair the broken vessels of our lives and make something pleasing to Himself. With great love and care He will redeem our brokenness.

If we will entrust ourselves to Him, He can do things that seem impossible. He can use our very brokenness to fashion a vessel that is pleasing in His sight. He can make us vessels of honor again.

Lord, though I am like a broken vessel, I trust You to fashion me into a vessel that is pleasing in Your sight.

Trust in Him at all times, you people.
Psalm 62:8

I imagined God having this conversation with the devastated, abused child in me:

"God."

"Yes, child."

"Do You really want me to trust You?"

"Yes, child, I do."

"God, how can I when my trust has been broken? How can I trust in You at all times?"

"Child, draw close to Me. Learn about Me and My everlasting love. Test My faithfulness. See that I am slow to anger. In time, you will come to believe that I will never leave you or forget you. Then you will be healed, and you will be able to trust in Me at all times."

Thank You, God. I'll try. Please help me.

Blessed is she who believed, for there will be fulfillment of those things which were told her from the Lord.
Luke 1:45

God talks to me in many ways. Sometimes I hear His voice in my heart. Other times He uses those around me to speak words of encouragement at just the right time. The things God tells me are hard to believe. The pain sometimes gets so great that I can hardly stand it, but He says He won't give me more than I can bear. He tells me that I am worthy of His love, but I struggle to accept that.

It's hard to believe anything good will come from my memories. But I have heard God say that the pain I've gone through is going to be used to help others. I choose to believe Him, not my fears.

Lord, give me the courage to believe You for my healing.

> *Is not the day of the LORD darkness,*
> *and not light?*
> *Is it not very dark, with no*
> *brightness in it?*   Amos 5:20

In the Old Testament the day of the Lord was usually a "dark" time of war or famine or some other kind of disaster. As survivors of abuse, we often feel we are living in darkness and wonder if God is angry with us.

But Christ spent a day of darkness in our place. He endured the cross for our sins and God judged Him in our place. No matter what our darkness has been, Jesus will bear it. I can place my darkness in Him.

Jesus, take away all my darkness.

> *The Spirit of the Lord GOD . . .*
> *has anointed Me . . .*
> *To console those who mourn in Zion,*
> *To give them beauty for ashes,*
> *The oil of joy for mourning.*
>
> Isaiah 61: 1, 3

Healing can never come unless first we mourn. Sexually abused women have much to mourn in the loss of innocence and childhood. The simple delights and games of children were lost to us too early. Our bodies learned responses and our hearts experienced feelings much too advanced for our ages. That which God intended as a beautiful gift one day to our spouses became instead a stumbling block that would set us on a journey of repeated victimization.

It is never too late for us to regain our lost childhood, but first we must recount the loss and mourn. Only when we empty out our lives can our Lord begin to refill them. Let us empty ourselves of the ashes of our past and allow Him to bestow upon us His gifts of beauty and joy.

Lord, help me to mourn the losses of the past so that I may receive Your comfort, beauty, and joy.

*I am the LORD; I will bring you out from under
  the burdens.*
Exodus 6:6

I sat and watched a small ant carrying a piece of
straw—such a huge burden for such a tiny creature!
The ant came to a wide crack in the sidewalk, too
wide for it to cross. It stood for a time as if wondering what to do. Then it laid the straw over the crack
and walked across to the other side.

That ant teaches us all a lesson. Being victims of
sexual abuse can seem to be a burden too huge for
us to carry. We have God's promise that He will
bring us out from under that burden. He alone can
turn that same burden into a blessing so that we,
too, may use it to reach the other side.

*Dear Father, bring me out from under the burdens of sexual
abuse and use them in my life as a bridge to blessing.*

> *A friend loves at all times,*
> *And a brother is born for*
> *adversity.*
>
> Proverbs 17:17

When my sexual abuse issues began to surface I had to deal with many things. One of the most painful was the loss of friendships. Friends said hurtful things like: "What do you mean, you have to work through this? Just pray, and God will heal you"; or "It's in the past. Put it behind you. Pull yourself together."

Perhaps you, too, have had friends who didn't understand what you were going through. Just remember, there is someone who does understand—Jesus.

He knows how it feels to be deserted by those we call friends. He understands our pain. We have His promise that He will not forsake us. He is a friend who will love us at all times, and in Him we find a brother who will share our adversity.

Thank You, Jesus, for being a friend who loves and understands at all times, especially in times of adversity.

*Then God said, "Let there be light"; and there
was light . . . and God divided the light from
the darkness.*

Genesis 1:3–4

God looks upon the dark recesses of our lives and
says, "Let there be light."

As we emerge from our victimization and abuse,
we are like treasures coming out of darkness (see
Isa. 45:3). God sees us with the same delight as a
miner who discovers gold or diamonds. He is not
put off by whatever roughness there may be because He knows we are of great value. He sees our
beauty and worth.

We need not fear His light or what it will expose.
He is simply fulfilling His promise to us: "For there is
nothing hidden which will not be revealed, nor has
anything been kept secret but that it should come to
light" (Mark 4:22).

*Thank You, Lord, for shining Your light into the darkness of my
secret places.*

> *Through the LORD's mercies we are*
> *not consumed,*
> *Because His compassions fail not.*
> *They are new every morning;*
> *Great is Your faithfulness.*
> Lamentations 3:22–23

There have been times when I felt totally consumed by the grief and shame of my past. It is easy to get lost and stuck in the pain of life. It helps to remember the progress that I have made and the changes that have taken place in my life since my healing began.

God's love has been a constant during this season in my life. I have not always been able to feel His presence, but I know that I have not been alone in this process.

Every day God is faithful to see me through the things I must face. When I lose sight of Him, I know I am in danger of being consumed. The issues that face me now are too big to handle on my own; they are more manageable when I can rely on His faithfulness.

———————————

Lord, I am counting on You to keep me from being consumed!

*He who has begun a good work in you will
complete it until the day of Jesus Christ.*

Philippians 1:6

The Answer

*I have my answer now!
My years of hanging on to pain;
Afraid of letting go of this old
    familiar friend.
Pain, I called you "friend."
Because without you
The emptiness became so real;
The desolation was unbearable.*

Working through the healing process involves facing painful issues such as anger, fear, and shame. Healing is not an easy path to choose. But the truth is, pain isn't your friend; Jesus is. Pain hangs on to you to keep you from the life to which God has called you. It keeps you from the joy that could be yours.

Take the time to journal the benefits you receive by holding on to pain. Then write out the reasons for saying goodbye.

Dear God, help me let go of the pain and realize the deceptions that keep me from Your completeness.

> *Do not be overcome by evil, but overcome evil with good.*
>
> Romans 12:21

The enemy has a way of making an evil thought or picture a constant torment if we don't address it and pray through to healing. One of the pictures sexually abused women are harassed with is an oversized, grotesque, or sword-like penis. It can cause great difficulties in the marriage bed. Of course, that is what the evil one desires.

To combat fear of the male genitals, ask the Lord to help you bring every thought captive and let truth reign. If need be, seek the aid of a trusted friend, biblical counselor, or pastor. It won't happen all at once. Just remember that once you heal those wounds, you can accept your partner's body. That acceptance will bring beauty to the marriage.

The good news is, good really can overcome evil.

Dear Lord, let me recognize the evil that is trying to overcome me. Bring me the good that will overcome the evil.

> *"For I will restore health to you*
> *And heal you of your wounds," says the LORD,*
> *"Because they called you an outcast."*
>
> Jeremiah 30:17

A sexually abused woman often acts out her pain through rage. She uses rage to control her environment, protecting herself from further abuse. But the rage repels those who desire to comfort, and the wounded woman can become an outcast even in her own community.

God is not offended or scared off by our rage. He understands the pain behind our actions, but He also desires to restore us to health. We cannot hang on to our rage and find restoration in God. We must allow Him to protect us through His healing ways.

Lord, restore me to health and take this rage far from me so that I will no longer be an outcast among Your people.

> *I am the good shepherd. The good shepherd
> gives His life for the sheep.*   John 10:11

The Good Shepherd gave His life for us on the cross. And because He did we can attain heaven. We won't attain it by any so-called good works that we might do, because they could never be good enough. Believing in Him is the only way; He is our provision. We have eternal life because the Good Shepherd gave His life for us.

And He is still giving His life for us. He is always active. Every day He gives us His life by bearing our burdens, healing our hearts, and interceding for us. He is the Good Shepherd.

Lord, be my Good Shepherd.

For you will forget the shame of your youth.
Isaiah 54:4

Many of us have pasts we would like to forget. The violation of my body at an early age prompted certain thoughts and feelings long before their proper time. Although the sexual abuse had been beyond my control, there came a point in my life when I took charge and used my sexuality.

After I came to know the Lord, I saw my past through His eyes. I wept in shame over the games I had played with my sexuality, using it to control others instead of treating it as God's precious gift. In the end, my behavior hurt me more than anyone.

I lifted every memory to the Lord, and as His forgiveness flowed, my shame dissipated through my tears.

Although we can't forget our pasts, through Jesus' touch we can release our shame. Then we will be free.

Lord, give me the courage to share, forgetting the shame of my youth.

> *Now if we are children, then we are heirs—heirs*
> *of God and co-heirs with Christ, if indeed we*
> *share in his sufferings in order that we may also*
> *share in his glory.*   Romans 8:17 NIV

I don't want to grow up and be like my mother!"

These words have echoed in my mind since I was fifteen. The pain I carried because of her lack of protection, love, and bonding marked my adult life. Often she spoke to me with words that said I was unimportant, unworthy to be a person or her daughter. She unwittingly reinforced the abuse and victimization from my stepfather. As an adult I found myself acting just like my mother, thinking, "like mother, like daughter."

Jesus came so that I might have a new lineage, be an heir of God and co-heir with Christ.

My hope of worthiness and security is now founded in my relationship with Jesus. He teaches what a loving, caring parent He is. I've changed because of Him.

Jesus, help me to continue to accept Your care and love toward me, not judging my mother or myself.

My soul, wait silently for God alone,
For my expectation is from Him.

Psalm 62:5

As I worked through my abuse, I had to face my relationship with my parents. I was deeply disappointed in them because I had expected them to meet my desperate need for love and approval. I struggled to accept this painful fact until I realized that only the Lord can fill those voids. As I surrendered my needs and expectations to Him, I found release from the turmoil in my soul.

Return to your rest, O my soul,
For the LORD has dealt bountifully with you.

He has drawn you with lovingkindness, and has loved you with an everlasting love. Your hope and expectation are fulfilled in Him. Return to your rest, O my soul (see Ps. 116:7; Jer. 31:3).

> *In the fear of the LORD there is strong confidence,*
> *And His children will have a place of refuge.*
>
> Proverbs 14:26

Father," I sighed, "I'm just not disciplined." He challenged me, "Think on your work day and all its discipline. Now consider why that doesn't carry over to your home."

As I meditated, two distinctly different personalities emerged from within me: successful, secure, and efficient at work; insecure, confused, and disorganized at home. The Lord explained, "The workplace has always been a place of affirmation for you; thus, you have confidence there. Use this revelation to set yourself free."

God wants our earthly homes to be reflections of our eternal home. He has promised His children a place of confidence and a place of refuge. As victims of abuse, we lived in homes that were probably unsafe, and any affirmation came from elsewhere. We can break that pattern by rejecting the lies of our past and bringing our affirmed selves into our homes.

_____

Father, I pray that my earthly home will reflect confidence and safety for me and my family.

> *And do not despise your mother when
> she is old.*   Proverbs 23:22

Love your mother as I love her," the Lord impressed upon my heart.

This was my first visit home in many years, a sort of reconciliation. As God had walked me through the painful issues of abuse, He also had healed the many related issues concerning my mother. Now, much as I wanted to restore our relationship, my words seemed to go nowhere.

One morning I felt compelled to give her a hug, and I gave her another that evening. This became our daily greeting and nightly parting gesture. The days that followed brought such a transformation in my mother, it could only have been from God. It was not the words spoken during my visit that made the difference, but the touch of the Lord through me.

God is a God of reconciliation. Let Him heal your broken relationships. If you're willing He is able.

Thank You, Jesus, for healing me so that I can love my mother again.

He will teach us His ways,
And we shall walk in His paths.

Isaiah 2:3

Childhood is a time to learn how relationships operate. I remember trying to figure out what would make men, especially my dad, interested in me. I was eleven years old and my dad was withdrawn from life in general and me in particular. I so wanted his love and attention.

One day, after seeing his interest in *Playboy* magazine, I looked at the pictures and vowed to be like the women pictured there so he would love me, too. In the years that followed, I used my body to fill the love hunger within me. It didn't work. I only felt more loneliness, and then I felt shame as well.

Jesus is the answer to the void in us. He promises to show us a way of living that will satisfy us. We must repent of the hurtful ways of the past and learn His ways.

_____

Lord, I repent of the harmful ways I tried to find love and acceptance. Forgive me and teach me Your ways.

> *He also brought me up out of*
>   *a horrible pit,*
> *Out of the miry clay,*
> *And set my feet upon a rock,*
> *And established my steps.*
>   Psalm 40:2

I was in a pit made by my father for more than thirty years. I didn't realize why I was depressed, angry, and fearful until I started remembering the shame and horror of his abuse.

Now I am climbing out of the pit one step at a time. Jesus is holding my hand and guiding my steps. I trust in Him, and I am growing stronger every day.

We all have our own "pits" we need to crawl out of: pits of abuse, neglect, defeat, and failure. God will guide our steps to victory through His Son, Jesus Christ, if we but ask Him.

Jesus, thank You for bringing me out of the pit and making my steps firm.

> *Let your conduct be without covetousness, and*
> *be content with such things as you have. For He*
> *Himself has said, "I will never leave you nor*
> *forsake you."*
>   Hebrews 13:5

Before I started my journey to healing I believed I could not live without a man. I thought my life could not be whole without a man. I feared that if he ever left me I couldn't make it.

Things changed and, sure enough, he left me, but God used the opportunity to prove Himself sufficient. His love was so constant I didn't care if I ever had a man in my life again.

God has promised to be my husband when I'm alone, and the perfect presence of the Holy Spirit develops an intimacy humans can't achieve. He never leaves me or disappoints me. I need nothing else but Him.

Thank You, Lord, that I covet only You, the source of true joy and contentment.

> *You have ravished my heart,*
> *My sister, my spouse;*
> *You have ravished my heart*
> *With one look of your eyes,*
> *With one link of your necklace.*
> Song of Solomon 4:9

Solomon wrote these words about his soon-to-be bride, Abishag. Even though Solomon had seven hundred wives and three hundred concubines, Abishag caught his eye. What is it about this kind of look? We've all seen it at one time or another, or experienced getting "the look," or giving "the look." There is a sensation or a vibration that sends an unspoken message.

My father sent me this message with "the look" at an early age. The vibration it caused was mixed with fear and curiosity. It sent chills up my spine, and vomit up my throat. It was clearly a sexual message, one I came to despise. Now it's hard to receive looks from my husband.

Father God, take away the painful memory of my father's look, heal my heart, and let me receive from my husband.

> *Yes, the Almighty will be your gold*
> *And your precious silver;*
> *For then you will have your*
> *   delight in the Almighty.*
>   Job 22:25–26

Pleasers live in the "performance" mode. We can do ten things at once and do them well. We delight in our reward—the approval of the audience—for it tells us who we are. We fear that if we stop doing, we will no longer be valued.

Within God, we can stop doing and still be His valued creation. We are unique personalities in unique bodies created with special gifts for special purposes.

We can discover our true value by seeing ourselves reflected in our Father's eyes. Gazing on God's face, we feel His love and no longer need an audience, for we have found the only reward we need . . . Him.

———————

Help me, Father, to stop seeking my reward in pleasing people.
You alone are my reward. You alone are more precious than silver and gold.

How precious also are Your thoughts to me,
O God!   Psalm 139:17

Lord, I owe You an apology. I spend a lot of time talking to You. I am constantly telling You what I think or feel, even though I know You already know. But I spend very little time listening to what You have to say. Lord, I'm sorry. Please forgive me.

As I read Your words today, Lord, let them be sweet to my ears. I long to know You better. Your thoughts are precious to me. I do want to hear what is on Your mind and what You have to say.

I know that only the truth can set me free. Your words are truth and life. Speak Your precious truth to me today, Lord.

Lord, our relationship is important to me. Your thoughts are precious to me. Speak, Lord, for Your servant listens.

The righteous shall flourish like a palm tree,
He shall grow like a cedar in Lebanon.

Psalm 92:12

Righteousness comes through the blood of Jesus Christ, and the Bible tells us that those who have received Him are righteous. This verse implies that they are like a long-living, tall, fruitful palm tree. They are also like the cedar tree which is strong and durable.

Both trees are able to live in the dry, hot desert. Insects will not attack cedar wood because of its hardness and scent. In old Jerusalem cedar wood was used to build the temple of God because of its strength.

I am so grateful that God has redeemed me and is making me flourish like these trees! For many years I was like a weed underfoot. I only knew the abusive hand of my earthly father. Now I am receiving the tender gardening of my heavenly Father. Under His care I am vital and growing. He is my sustainer and wonderful gardener!

Thank You, Lord, for making me flourish.

> *To everything there is a season,*
> *A time for every purpose under heaven. . . .*
> *A time to weep, and a time to laugh;*
> *A time to mourn, and a time to dance.*
>
> Ecclesiastes 3:1, 4

School was in session, and I was learning difficult lessons. I was a basket case, restless, crying, in pain. I suffered as hurts were revealed and responses healed. Then suddenly God gave me a respite, a summer vacation. He gave me two months of much happiness, confidence in His promises, and joyful acceptance of who I am.

In His mercy, God varies our seasons so we can walk through our healing as He reveals to us.

Let us embrace each new season. Let us see our pasts, understand the present, and be free to walk forth into the future without fear, trusting that our seasons are in His hands.

Thank You, Lord of our seasons. Your perfect timing prepares us for each new phase and leads us into greater truth and joy.

*The harvest truly is plentiful, but the laborers
are few. Therefore pray the Lord of the harvest
to send out laborers into His harvest.*

Matthew 9:37–38

Harvest time! The ripened crops are gathered, and
the storehouses are full and brimming over! Old traditions of harvest festivals have become new again.
People have rejected the demonic origins of Hallow-
een and celebrate instead the joys of our loving and
generous God, the Lord of the harvest!

Jesus said the fields are ripe, and the crops are
ready to be gathered. As survivors of sexual abuse,
we see other wounded women who need to be
brought home to the Lord for healing and wholeness. More workers are needed to go into the fields
and tell the suffering that there is hope and healing,
there is worth and value, there is a future in the
Lord Jesus.

At this harvest season let us respond to the challenge and answer God's call. Let us go forth to those
who are in such need.

Lord, make me a worthy laborer in Your harvest. Lord, send me.

HANDS OF MEN

He had no idea what he'd done,
his evil violation,
the violent murder of my soul.

He carved away all trust,
thrust his body's sword within me,
spilt his seed, and left me dead,
yet breathing.

It was not my will
to have my senses stirred,
to be stripped of innocence.
I've felt like a beggar on the streets,
searching for the scraps of a person,
filled with shame and sorrow,
thunderous rage,
and a woman's poisoned cry
for love . . .

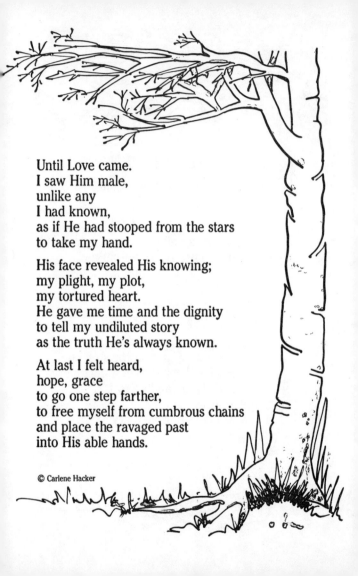

Until Love came.
I saw Him male,
unlike any
I had known,
as if He had stooped from the stars
to take my hand.

His face revealed His knowing;
my plight, my plot,
my tortured heart.
He gave me time and the dignity
to tell my undiluted story
as the truth He's always known.

At last I felt heard,
hope, grace
to go one step farther,
to free myself from cumbrous chains
and place the ravaged past
into His able hands.

I am the Lord who heals you.
Exodus 15:26

The Lord our healer is Jehovah Rapha. *Rapha* in Hebrew means "to mend"; the implication is to mend by stitching or sewing together.

When God called Himself Jehovah Rapha, He was declaring that He is the One who mends us. He alone will sew together hearts and lives that have been ripped apart. Jehovah Rapha, the Lord our healer, will be the patient, skillful tailor in our lives.

Our part of this healing process is to recognize that we are like damaged garments, unable to mend ourselves. Just as a garment must be flexible and cooperative in a tailor's hands, so we too must be in God's hands. Like a torn garment, we can be made as good as new if we allow our healer, Jehovah Rapha, to do His mending.

Thank You, Lord, for being Jehovah Rapha to me. Heal me, Lord, and sew my life together as You see fit.

> *Jesus has become a surety of a better covenant.*
>
> Hebrews 7:22

Many survivors of abuse have made earthly covenants with people, things, or even themselves. These unholy choices can include food, drugs, alcohol, and even men. These things enslave and entrap us. There is only One, Jesus, who can make a perfect covenant to fulfill our needs in a better, healthier way. He guaranteed it, by giving His own life for us (John 3:16).

Jesus, help me to see that the earthly covenants I have made are self-defeating and that You are the only perfect One with whom to make a covenant.

Make me to hear joy and gladness,
That the bones which You have broken
  may rejoice.   Psalm 51:8

The sound of a shepherd's voice has a calming effect on his sheep, who will usually gather near him for protection and care. When a contrary sheep continually strays from the protection of the flock, a shepherd will break its leg to restrict it. While the leg heals the shepherd tenderly cares for the sheep, even carrying it across his shoulders as the flock moves from place to place. The sheep becomes bonded to the shepherd and wants to remain very close even after the leg is healed.

God will allow in our lives whatever "broken bones" are necessary to bond us to Him. He promises to carry us through the mending process. We will hear with joy and gladness His voice calling us back to His protection. We will rejoice in our "broken bones."

_____

Lord, teach me to rejoice in my "broken bones."

Those who sow in tears
Shall reap in joy.
Psalm 126:5

I don't even remember when I made a vow not to cry. I had been embarrassed many times by people's harsh responses to my tears: "You're too sensitive!" or "If you weren't so emotional, we would get along better!" It was true that I often overreacted because of my woundedness, but it hurt even more to hear it. Not knowing what else to do, I began to deny all emotions by burying them. I became hard.

I was in my thirties when I gave my life to the Lord. He soon tapped into that well of stuffed tears and there seemed no way to stop them. Joy overflowed from the relief, and I was on the road to healing!

Woundedness often leaves us emotionally stuck. Releasing our tears is a way to allow our emotions to heal so that we might experience the joy of wholeness.

Thank You, Lord, for giving me back the gift of tears that allowed me to experience the joy of healing.

> *My tears have been my food day and night,*
> *While they continually say to me,*
> *"Where is your God?"*
>
> Psalm 42:3

My tears are like a cloudburst on a summer's day that strikes with fury and then suddenly goes away. The clouds gather quickly, bursting forth like the summer storm. Always echoing like wind in the storm is the haunting question, "Where is God?"

The Lord has already answered my question:

> *Fear not, for I am with you;*
> *Be not dismayed, for I am*
> *your God.*
>
> (Isa. 41:10a)

> *When you pass through the*
> *waters, I will be with you;*
> *And through the rivers, they*
> *shall not overflow you.*
>
> (Isa. 43:2)

> *Yes, I will help you,*
> *I will uphold you with My*
> *righteous right hand.*
>
> (Isa. 41:10b)

Thank You, Lord, for being with me, for strengthening me, and for helping me.

> *Do not say, "Why were the former days better
> than these?" For you do not inquire wisely
> concerning this.*
>   Ecclesiastes 7:10

I was content living at home, until God abruptly moved me out. At first I was heartbroken—it seemed better the other way. As time passed I adjusted, growing deeper in my knowledge of Him. I would have gladly spent the rest of my life there in that intimate place alone with Him.

Then God moved me back home again. I grieved through the difficult period of readjustment, saying, "Why, Lord? It was better when there was just You and me."

Again I had to realize I had given God control of my life. He is wiser than I am. I must trust that He is orchestrating the changes in my life to move me to a better place. I must not hold on to the past.

Help me, Lord, not to look back but to move forward in anticipation, believing the best is yet to come.

*For he found her in the countryside, and the
betrothed young woman cried out, but there
was no one to save her.* Deuteronomy 22:27

It was a cloudy morning, and I had slept in later
than usual. My neighborhood classmates had already left for school, so that meant I would have to
walk alone. As I frantically hurried along I came to a
crosswalk. Without hesitation I stepped into it, only
to be cut off by a blue, low-built car. Suddenly the
door opened and I was snatched into the car. In desperation I cried out, but there was no one to save
me. I never made it to school that day, and I told no
one of the rape.

Twenty years later this deep secret surfaced as if
it had happened yesterday. Going through steps of
recovery, I found that I was not alone. God heard me
cry out, felt the pain, and never wanted it to happen. It wasn't God's fault; it was the sin of a man.

God, continue to heal my heart.

> *I said in my haste,*
> *"All men are liars."*
> Psalm 116:11

When we were growing up we made judgments we carried into adulthood. We decided that all men were liars, untrustworthy and unreliable. We couldn't count on them. Our judgments often extended to God too, since He was seen as a man.

Let us reevaluate our hasty judgments against men and God. It is true that people, including ourselves, will never be totally reliable, honest, or pure in motive. But that does not mean all men are liars. Let us also separate God from man. God is perfect, doesn't lie, and doesn't make mistakes.

When we allow ourselves to be vulnerable to God and others who care, the blessing of His Presence in us will transform our abused hearts. We can take people's imperfections in stride as we shift our trust to the Perfect One.

Lord, help me to reject my childhood judgments of men and of You. I open my heart to You and I accept people as You accept me.

And the king was exceedingly sorry; yet,
because of the oaths and because of those who
sat with him, he did not want to refuse her.

Mark 6:26

King Herod had respect for John the Baptist, knowing he was a holy man sent by God. Nevertheless, the king chose to kill the prophet to avoid being embarrassed, even though he was sorry! He carried out this evil deed because he was afraid of others' disapproval. Like so many others, he refused to live according to God's law. The price he paid for his evil living was family tension, jealousy, murder, and judgment by Almighty God. God is the righteous judge of all men who are evil.

Maybe you have endured the foolish choices of evil men. Perhaps you have been destroyed by a powerful man. Can you turn that evil man over to the righteous judge today?

Lord, I release _____ to You today, acknowledging that You are his judge, not me.

Be angry, and do not sin.
Psalm 4:4

At age two my son learned he could increase water pressure in the backyard hose by kinking the end momentarily and then releasing it. Much to his delight, he discovered that with this newfound weapon he could squirt the cat at great distances. The cat, of course, was not so delighted.

Unresolved anger puts a similar kink in the flow of our purpose in God. We may be outwardly performing good deeds, but the pressure behind our anger can cause us to act inappropriately, and no one wants to be on the receiving end. The anger we feel may be righteous, but only God can be trusted with its resolution.

Jesus, I give You my anger so that I will no longer hinder Your purpose in my life.

*Bearing with one another, and forgiving one
another . . . even as Christ forgave you,
so you also must do.* Colossians 3:13

We'll be there tomorrow," my mother-in-law informed me. I felt victimized again. She didn't care what I thought, and it hurt. I dreaded her three-week visit.

In the past, I had always ended up in bed by the time she left. This time, though, I finally came before the Lord. I began to journal all the things my mother-in-law had done that wounded me deeply, and I knew I needed to forgive her for her actions. My tears began to flow as I read page after page, and with every tear my pain diminished.

When my mother-in-law arrived, she was my new friend. I had moved from my victim role to a role as active forgiver. Forgiveness allowed me to accept her.

Lord, thank You for forgiving me and leading me to forgiveness of others.

Seek good and not evil,
That you may live;
So the Lord God of hosts will
be with you,
As you have spoken.

Amos 5:14

God sent Amos the shepherd to the people of Israel to warn them of God's anger against them. He preached to them about doing what was right, and he told them that God loved all the people and wanted justice for them. He knew God cares very much for people who are afflicted and treated unfairly.

This verse encourages me that God is a God of justice and will be the judge of those who have abused me. I do not have to carry the burden of making my perpetrator pay for what he did to me. This relieves me of a lifetime of trying to get even. This allows me to let go so that God can take over.

Lord, my only goodness comes from You. I release my need for justice to You.

> *But we have this treasure in earthen vessels,*
> *that the excellence of the power may be of*
> *God and not of us.*   2 Corinthians 4:7

Archaeologists have found treasures of silver and gold inside some of the cheap clay pots used in biblical times. The pots themselves were dull, broken, and worthless, but hidden inside were priceless valuables.

Survivors of sexual abuse are like those pots. We may feel broken, useless, and hopeless, but God wants to be the excellent power within us. He is the treasure and we are the vessels. He makes us valuable and special.

Dear God, I offer You myself as I am, wounded and weak. Please fill me with the priceless treasure of Your presence.

> *Fill their faces with shame*
> *That they may seek Your*
> *name, O LORD.*
> Psalm 83:16

Positive shame—the words startled me. Had I heard God right? Shame is such an issue in the lives of victims. Much of our journey to recovery is spent learning how to overcome shame, be cleansed of it, and not take it on again. How, then, could the Lord Himself use the word?

I began to search the Scriptures and was surprised to see how often shame is used in just the way He had used it with me. Remember without ownership, there can be no positive shame and no repentance.

Ah, positive shame—the real thing, not false shame—the stuff most abused women carry around for years. Positive shame is about recognizing our common sins. When we do that, we are rightly ashamed before God and seek Him in true repentance.

Holy Spirit, convict me of my sins and bring me to a place of positive shame and true repentance that I may seek forgiveness and change my ways.

Blessed be the LORD,
Who has not given us as prey
* to their teeth.*
Our soul has escaped as a bird
* from the snare of the fowlers;*
The snare is broken, and we
* have escaped.*

Psalm 124:6–7

Shame haunts victims of sexual abuse. Their bodies and their emotions often betray them. A little girl, starved for Daddy's attention, often settles for the only "affection" she can get. How can she deny her body's pleasurable response to his touch? Because of her need she takes responsibility for each encounter; she does not know how to stop it. Shame traps her when she believes the lie that the abuse is her fault.

Jesus wants to set us free from this lie. As victims, we were not responsible for our abuse. Jesus knows that the abusers are the guilty ones.

Jesus, release me from the snare of shame and guilt that is not mine.

> *He chose us in Him before the foundation of*
> *the world, that we should be holy and without*
> *blame before Him in love.*   Ephesians 1:4

I can't remember ever feeling accepted. I was born the wrong sex at the wrong time, and my family didn't want me. Then I was sexually abused, and my battle with rejection escalated. I felt that if my friends knew the darkness within me, they would be repulsed. God wouldn't even want me. How could I drag my dirty, shameful, lonely soul into the presence of His holiness? How could He touch me?

Then one day God revealed that the beliefs I had were totally opposed to the reality of His grace and mercy. I was denying His redemption and restoration.

We are not born by accident. God had a purpose and plan for us before the world began. In His sight we are holy and blameless. Thinking otherwise is denying His love.

_____

Thank You, Lord, for choosing me and restoring me to holiness by Your love.

Since you were precious in My sight,
You have been honored,
And I have loved you.   Isaiah 43:4

Abuse wipes out the innocence of youth, but God can restore it! When I was a little girl, one of my cherished memories was sitting on my grandmother's lap and listening to her recite poetry. As I climbed down she would say, "I love you, precious." I would think about the word *precious* as I snuggled under my covers.

One night I stayed with a favorite cousin who molested me, stealing something precious from me. Grandma continued to call me "precious," but it never felt quite the same.

Years later I read in Scripture that the Father saw me as precious. I crawled up on His lap. He wiped my tears and said, "I love you, precious." At that moment I was cleansed, renewed!

Thank You, Lord, for seeing me as Your precious child.

For God has not given us a spirit of fear, but
of power and of love and of a sound mind.
                                                2 Timothy 1:7

As victims we often feel out of control, insecure, vulnerable, and fundamentally deficient. A key to overcoming these feelings is to renew our relationship with the Word by meditating on what God says.

God is love, and His perfect love casts out all fear (see 1 John 4:8, 18).

We are the apple of His eye, imbued with the power of His Spirit (see Ps. 17:8; Acts 1:8).

He has promised us that if we keep our thoughts on Him, He will give us peace of mind (see Isa. 26:3).

Thank You, Lord, for giving me power, love, and a sound mind. Help me resist the fear today.

But as for me, I would seek God,
And to God I would commit my cause—
Who does great things, and unsearchable,
Marvelous things without number.

Job 5:8–9

The great things God does allow me to look back over my pain and heartbreak and say sincerely, "I am deeply and forever grateful." When I committed my past to God, He did marvelous things in me, things that transformed me from a victim into a victor.

He provided a safe place for me to relive the nightmare, to release the pain, and then to renew my mind. Because of that I am closer today to what God made me to be: honest, unafraid, compassionate, vulnerable, living life to the fullest.

I would not have known the fruit of suffering and sorrow had I not felt them in my depths, for it is only when we are free to feel our pain that we are released to feel joy.

I committed my cause to You, dear God, and You did marvelous things in me and for me. I am forever grateful.

> *Do not remember the former things,*
> *Nor consider the things of old.*
> *Behold, I will do a new thing.*
> Isaiah 43:18–19

Behold, I will do a new thing." What a beautiful promise! God has given us something to really hang on to as we struggle to let go of the past. We should acknowledge the abuse that occurred, and then we can let it go, move on, and allow God to do new things with our lives.

There is excitement and life in this promise. We no longer have to be stuck in the past; we can eagerly look to the future and the marvelous surprises God has waiting for us.

Help me not to dwell on things of the past, but to eagerly look forward to the new life You are creating for me. Thank You, Father.

Yet You have brought up my life from the pit,
O Lord, my God.
Jonah 2:6

Dare to prepare for the best and it might happen to you."

When I heard a mother say this to her teenage daughter, I could not help but think of my past. I had not prepared for the best. While other girls prepared for their futures through education, I lived promiscuously. But God, through His mercy and love for me, brought me up from the pit.

Now through healing, restoration, and education in God's Word and His ways, I can help other women like me. It doesn't matter where we start; it only matters where we finish. God can bring us out of the pit and into the future He has prepared. It can happen to us!

Thank You, Lord, for taking me from the pit and restoring my future. Use me to help others.

*Yea, though I walk through
the valley of the shadow
of death,
I will fear no evil.*

Psalm 23:4

I was abused as a small child, but I had no conscious memories until years later. The first memories were quick flashes, more like imaginations than real memories. As the floodgates of remembering opened I went back to the past, where all of the horror engulfed me.

Walking through the shadows of our past is scary and feels overpowering. We need to remember they are only shadows of what has been. We need fear no evil, because the Lord will never allow the darkness to overwhelm us. He is there with us even when we don't see Him.

Lord, help me to remember You are with me in the shadows of my past and that I have nothing to fear.

For you shall go out with joy,
And be led out with peace.
Isaiah 55:12

As we deal with memories of our sexual abuse, we fear we may never experience true joy or peace again. We try to function on a day-to-day basis the best way we can, but the pain and torment are never far from us.

We desperately need God's help! We must learn to trust Him in ways we have not known before. We must risk believing He does love and value us. We must be willing to let Him show us how to overcome the past. Then we shall go out into the world with joy, and we will be led in peace from painful memories.

_____

Lord, help me let go of my fears and trust You to bring me forth in peace and joy.

> *Then he said to him, "Come home with me*
> *and eat bread."*
>   1 Kings 13:15

This verse is taken from the story of King Jeroboam, but it reminds me of going home to eat with my family. For weeks before Thanksgiving I would feel nauseated in anticipation of the visit. I would stand in card shops looking for appropriate cards to win the approval of my family. I always picked the most flattering ones, because there were none that said, *"Thanksgiving really grieves me—It reminds me of my childhood."* I would pray to God and ask Him to take away the sick feelings I had. Then I would add, "And please, God, don't let me be left alone with my dad."

Even as an adult, I feared my father's look, his voice, his touch. Thanksgiving dinner was always the same—Dad was in control of everything. Then one day, I faced him and told him how I felt. Guess what? I never again have to be afraid to go home for Thanksgiving.

_____

Lord, I have come home to You full of Thanksgiving.

> *Be anxious for nothing, but in everything by*
> *prayer and supplication, with thanksgiving, let*
> *your requests be made known to God.*
>
> Philippians 4:6

Thanksgiving is more than a season; it's a lifestyle. Although there are seasons in our lives when we can readily name our blessings, there are other times when being thankful is the farthest thing from our minds. We may be going through a difficult phase of our healing, reliving the pain of the sexual abuse and hurting so badly we wish we'd never begun the process.

Thanksgiving acknowledges God's purpose in our lives, in bad times and good. Focusing on His character gives us hope. We establish His Lordship through the expression of our continued trust in Him; our faith swells as we anticipate the fruits of the healing He is working in us.

At this time of the year let us commit to walking in praise and thanksgiving every day of our lives.

Lord, help me to live thankfully instead of anxiously.

> *For You have delivered my soul*
> *   from death,*
> *My eyes from tears,*
> *And my feet from falling.*
> *I will walk before the LORD*
> *In the land of the living.*
>
> Psalm 116:8–9

I have been transformed by the Lord's presence on the road to recovery. Now it's time to close this chapter of my life and start a new page. I am both sad and excited, for I have no idea what the future holds.

Not quite ready to leave the safety of familiarity, I lag behind my Lord. He is already leaping forth into the time of reaping and rejoicing He has promised. Trusting, I hang on for dear life so I won't be left behind.

I have many questions, but I sense the futility of asking them! I make just one request as we go forth together: "Finish what You have begun, Lord. Make me into what You have envisioned all along."

Thank You for delivering my soul from the past and for leading me into my future.

But those who wait on the LORD
Shall renew their strength. . . .
They shall walk and not faint.
Isaiah 40:31

How many times on our journey to wholeness do we hit an invisible brick wall? Bam! Down we go again! Each time it's more difficult to get up and walk again. Discouragement and hopelessness tell us there is no point in continuing.

In those moments, if we listen, we can also hear the voice of the psalmist saying: "I would have lost heart, unless I had believed that I would see the goodness of the LORD in the land of the living." " I will walk before the LORD in the land of the living" (Pss. 27:13; 116:9).

It is through waiting on the Lord and putting our hope and trust in Him that we exchange our strength for His. In that exchange we become renewed. Then we can continue to walk, and we will not faint.

Lord, I will wait on You. Please exchange my weariness for Your strength so I can continue my walk to wholeness.

> *I would have lost heart, unless I had believed*
> *That I would see the goodness of the LORD*
> *In the land of the living.*   Psalm 27:13

Even deep into our recovery, we can find ourselves in the midst of an unexpected battle with our abusers. Recoiling from a surprise attack, we may be tempted to give up. We can become discouraged, finding that the battle still rages hotter than ever. It is easy to lose heart.

Let us look beyond the circumstances. The enemy is always on the prowl, trying to undo the changes he sees in our lives. But God ensures our victory if we will continue the fight with His boldness and strength.

Let us once again take up our weapons in faith, believing that we will indeed see the goodness of the Lord reigning triumphant in our lives.

Dear Lord, help me not to lose heart on the road to my recovery. I am confident that Your goodness will reign supreme.

And if Christ is in you, the body is dead because of sin, but the Spirit is life because of righteousness.

Romans 8:10

In this chapter of Romans the apostle Paul writes about life in Christ. Many survivors of sexual abuse feel like their bodies are dead because of the sins committed against them. I know that there were times when I did not want to be alive. Life was not attractive to me; death seemed better.

This verse tells me that the Spirit gives me life because Christ lives in me. Christ's righteousness can lift me above this earthly body. He can lift me above the pain, above the abuse, above death, above sin. I have found life in Christ's righteousness because I have no righteousness of my own. In my recovery I am rejoicing because the Spirit of God has breathed life into me. I want to live every day now.

Jesus, please cover me with Your righteousness and give me life.

> *He has put a new song*
> *in my mouth—*
> *Praise to our God!*
> Psalm 40:3

As I look back over the road to my healing, I see how Jesus was there in every way. He was present even from that very first moment of pain, when everything seemed so hopelessly out of control. Jesus was there, enveloping me in His arms and holding me close.

I found peace in His presence and rest in His love. Finally I was able to trust Him enough to begin the process of healing. Just as He has been present from the start, I know He will be there for me to the end. What was once a ballad of mourning and despair is now a melody of discovering His faithfulness day by day.

Lord, my heart belongs to You! Your love surrounds me, and I am swept into Your presence. I am lost in Your love. Praises spill forth to my God, for I have discovered His faithfulness.

Thank You, Lord, for giving me a new love song. It was Your presence that got me through.

HOPE

It may begin as
a pinpoint of light
in my dark hour,
another rising of the sun,
a smile warm with safety,
someone who understands
my timid, "No."

From anywhere
within my small universe,
hope beckons me,
waiting, wanting
my response.
Once I see it,
I see Him,
offering me a life-line.

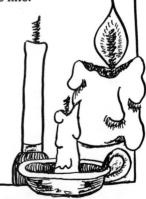

I am the light of the world. He who follows Me shall not walk in darkness, but have the light of life.
John 8:12

In Sweden, where I grew up, the days were so very short in December that by mid-afternoon nighttime darkness had descended. I always marveled at how the darkness immediately began to dissipate when the first Advent candle was lit in our home. After that every Sunday we lit one more candle as we anticipated Christmas. Our home grew brighter and brighter in those dark, dark days, bright with the light of Jesus Christ.

We live a continual Advent as we experience our healing process. In the darkest recesses of our minds lie the painful memories of sexual abuse. But as God heals us candles are lit, one by one, as we walk through healing, until the light of the Lord overcomes all the darkness.

As this Advent season culminates in our celebration of Jesus' birth, let us eagerly approach our own rebirth, for Jesus has made us new.

Lord, You are the light of my life.

*Daughter, be of good comfort; thy faith hath
made thee whole.* Matthew 9:22 KJV

A daughter is a precious gift from heaven, a bundle of sweetness, joy, and hope filled with love. A daughter is an honor and a blessing to cherish, protect, and nurture. A daughter needs gentleness as well as strength, understanding as well as discipline, guidance as well as freedom.

Hold a daughter softly; listen with your heart as well as your ears; dare to touch her soul by speaking kindly and sharing yourself honestly.

Our heavenly Father loves us in just this way, even when our earthly fathers don't. We are far more valuable to Him than we can comprehend. We must be strong in our faith and not accept the lies we've been told by those who did not see us with eyes like the Father's.

Father, we take comfort in Your love for us.

> *So God created man in His own image . . . male and female He created them.*   Genesis 1:27

I never understood what it meant to be made in God's image. I didn't know that to want more of life wasn't selfish, that to want my life to count for something good wasn't arrogant, that achieving and creating are parts of God's character, and He made us to be like Him.

As victims of sexual abuse we often shut down the parts of ourselves that would allow us to be the most we can be. Sometimes we've actually been told we are nobodies, and sometimes we just feel that we are. Knowing Jesus can set us free to be what we were created to be.

As the Lord revealed the truth, I rejoiced that I had been created with care and dignity to be all He wants me to be. I was free!

Lord, thank You that I am created in Your image to achieve and create, to count for good.

Do not fear, for you will not be ashamed;
Nor be disgraced, for you will not be
*   put to shame.*   Isaiah 54:4

There were times when I wanted to hide and not allow anyone to see the real me. The shame of my past caused me to close myself off. When I sat I covered my body with my hands, arms, or items I could hold. The more I could cover myself, the less shame I felt. It was that way in my relationships, too. I was always hiding, afraid to reveal myself because of shame.

In prayer I asked, "Is there no hope for me? Will my past always hinder my future?"

"No," a still small voice answered. "As you open your arms to hold others, I will cover your shame."

O Lord, thank You for Your promise to cover the shame of my past. Make me a vessel of Your healing to help others who hurt.

> *Awake to righteousness and do not sin; for some do not have the knowledge of God. I speak this to your shame.*   1 Corinthians 15:34

My shame tells me I am unimportant, stupid, and lazy. It says I am clumsy and will never amount to anything, because I can never be good enough. My shame tells me I am ugly and boring and have nothing good to offer anyone. It says I can never do anything right. It says I am unlovable and not worthy of respect.

But the shame is not mine and it does not bear my name. It belongs to my earthly father, who forced himself on me from the time I was three.

For so long I believed the lies, but no longer! My Father in heaven has awakened me to His righteousness. He sent His son to redeem me from this curse and He gives me honor instead of shame.

Father, thank You for the gift of Your Son, Jesus, and thank You for not shaming me.

And the LORD set a mark on Cain.
Genesis 4:15

I felt as if a word was stamped on my forehead in large wavy letters: *incest.* Never mind my intense longings, my hunger for lasting relationships, my desire to bond with someone special. Those God-given needs were the very ones I hated most in myself. Vowing self-protection, I lived alone with my shame and contempt behind walls of pain and fear.

Then Jesus sent to me a kind, understanding, wise counselor, who willingly invested her time, prayers, and love in me. Through her words of hope and healing, God breathed on my spirit and I began to live.

We who have been abused often feel marked for rejection. But God's mark on Cain was for the purpose of saving his life. God desires to save our lives from loneliness and shame. Let us wholeheartedly receive those whom He sends as reflections of His love.

Father, thank You that, as You did with Cain, You took steps to save my life.

> *Keep falsehood and lies far from me . . .*
> *But give me only my daily bread.*
>
> Proverbs 30:8 NIV

Many of us who have been sexually abused struggle with our weight. Some of us look to food for comfort, and some gain weight in order not to appear sexy. By looking unattractive and unappealing, we avoid the intimacy that causes so much pain. Avoidance also allows us to continue denying our pasts. Avoiding truth keeps us from being all that God made us to be.

Our dependence on food can be broken when we are able to shed the falsehoods and lies we have lived with in our denial. We can go to the Lord for healing. We can let Him turn everything in our pasts to His good, for His purpose in our lives.

Dear Jesus, thank You for removing the lies and healing me in order that I might need only my daily bread.

*And the man and his wife were both naked
and were not ashamed.*   Genesis 2:25 NASV

I knew that being uncomfortable with my body stemmed from the molestation I had suffered as a child. I looked back and realized how often that shame came into play. Physical education classes, dates, and even slumber parties caused me discomfort. My molester had mocked my breasts, and his words flashed through my head when I undressed or was close to someone.

A friend told me the Lord wants us to be naked and unashamed. Her advice was to stand naked in front of a mirror each day for thirty days and thank the Lord for His creation. I decided to try it.

The first week was painful and filled with tears. In the second week I realized how much I hated my body. In the third week I thought about the hurting words of my molester and asked God to remove them. In the last week I actually began to thank God that I was His creation.

It was a "de-shaming" process, and eventually it extended throughout all the areas of my life. The breakthrough for me began with my body. Where do you need to begin?

———————

Dear God, give me the grace to accept my body and to erase the shame. Enable me to stand before You unashamedly naked.

Be angry, and do not sin.
Psalm 4:4

It is not enough for us to learn how to channel anger constructively, for simply modifying our behaviors will not keep us from sinning.

We need to recognize that our anger is usually symptomatic of unresolved issues and wounds. The hidden pain we haven't faced fuels the anger. Until we get to the underlying causes we will continue to be angry. And no matter how hard we try to channel our anger, we will probably sin in the process.

To resolve our anger we must invite the Lord to reveal and heal the issues of our hearts. We may need to repent and forgive. We may also need to acknowledge patterns of thinking or responding that must be changed. Ultimately, only His touch on our hurts will enable us to be angry and not sin and finally allow Him to dissipate our anger and make us whole.

Lord, heal the hurts of my heart and resolve the source of my anger.

The counsel of the LORD stands forever,
The plans of His heart to all generations.
Psalm 33:11

Looking back at my parents and ancestors, I saw evidence that the Lord had sought them to walk with Him. None did. Instead of heeding His counsel my family had turned their backs, causing the same sexual sins to plague our family for generations.

In the pain of sexual abuse, the Lord sought me. How grateful I am that I listened as He revealed His plans for my family. He showed me that just one person yielding to Him and His ways can change those generational patterns and set the family free.

Let us respect the counsel of the Lord and answer His call. He will heal and restore not just us, but also our families and the generations that will follow us.

Lord, thank You for restoring me and my future generations to the plans of Your heart.

December 11

*Flee sexual immorality. Every sin that a man
does is outside the body, but he who commits
sexual immorality sins against his own body.*
1 Corinthians 6:18

Why was it so hard to accept my husband's love?
No matter how much he told me he loved me, I
didn't believe it. At times I would even provoke him
to reject me. My heart's desire had been fulfilled
with a husband, yet I couldn't trust him.

As I learned about sexual sin I saw what I had
done to myself and my marriage. After the abuse I
had vowed to get even. I had used men as they had
used me. The sexual encounters that followed kept
me from bonding with and embracing my husband.
The men in my past were like ghosts in our bed-
room.

The Lord brought each name and face before me
one by one, and I repented of my sin. He healed me
and restored the precious intimacy between my
husband and me.

*Lord, help me take responsibility and repent of my sexual sin, so
that its effect will no longer hinder me.*

> Bless the LORD . . .
> Who forgives all your
>   iniquities.
>   Psalm 103:2–3

After my father was released from the sanitarium, he was meaner than ever. He demanded that I be "good" to him. Terrified, I let him do whatever he wanted to me. Later, tiring of the struggles and of always being hurt, I gave up. I lost the will to live.

Years later I knelt and sobbed, "What's wrong with me, Lord?" He gently took me back to the incidents that had so traumatically affected me. I saw my sin: I had hardened my heart, not believing that God could ever be there for me. I repented as I realized His constant love. He forgave, cleansed, and set me free.

God is there for us, no matter what happens. Let us never give up. We can find life-giving hope in His eternal love and forgiveness.

You forgave my sins, O Lord, and I am forever grateful.

> *Now the purpose of the commandment is [to]*
> *love from a pure heart, from a good*
> *conscience, and from sincere faith.*
>
> 1 Timothy 1:5

Sexually abused? Me? Never!"

But wait! Many of us are codependent victims of a sexually addicted spouse. Both codependents and addicts come from dysfunctional homes and regenerate this dysfunction in their own homes. The addict seeks comfort from pain and stress in sex. The codependent tries to avoid pain by doing everything possible to keep the relationship together, despite the immoral behavior of the addict. Both think sex equals love.

Our heavenly Father weeps as He watches us, because we have corrupted the purity of love. If we seek to know God in sincere faith, He will show us that our corrupted kind of love is not from pure hearts and cannot rest in good consciences. We need to look to Him for wisdom in dealing with dysfunctional love. We must trust the Creator to give us the answers.

Lord, help me to know Your love and teach me how I should love my husband. Heal my family.

> *Delight yourself also in the LORD,*
> *And He shall give you the desires*
> *of your heart.* Psalm 37:4

What's the payoff?" the counselor asked me. I looked puzzled. She explained that we put up with abuse to get what we need in return—that's the payoff.

"Why do you keep taking his abuse? What are you afraid of losing?"

She made me face the terms of the unspoken contract. "I will endure your abuse so that I can still: play the game . . . be taken care of . . . maintain the image of a happy family. . . ."

God's contract is totally different. He wants us to have the desires of our hearts, and all we have to do is delight in Him! Let us renounce the unspoken contracts we have entered into that say, "I will suffer your abuse if you will give me whatever else I need." Let us instead enter joyfully into agreement with the Lord. It's easy to delight in Him, and whatever He gives us will fulfill our deepest desires.

Thank You, Lord, for giving me true love.

And being in agony, He prayed more earnestly.
And His sweat became like great drops of blood
falling down to the ground.   Luke 22:44

Because Jesus was fully human, He really does know how much we hurt. Even though He was also fully God, during His earthly life He experienced the same array of negative emotions we do—anger, grief, disappointment. He understands our feelings.

He also knows our limits better than we do, and He knows what to do when we are broken, weary, and empty. He yearns to renew us with His love. It is safe for us to open our hearts and believe Him. We can accept His love, His healing balm, His reassurance that everything's all right.

Let us not deny ourselves the consolation of the Lord's presence when we hurt. He too has felt the agony of betrayal, and His compassion flows from His own pain.

Lord, thank You for enduring agony here on earth and saving me. I can relate to You in my pain and let You heal me.

*Blessed be the God . . . who comforts us in all
our tribulation, that we may be able to comfort
those who are in any trouble, with the comfort
with which we ourselves are comforted by God.*
2 Corinthians 1:3–4

A child who has been sexually abused often turns
to masturbation. This happens because the nerves
that God created to be stimulated in the marriage
bed were aroused prematurely. Masturbation can
become a false comfort that a woman may struggle
with throughout her life. We can use many things to
comfort us falsely: food, alcohol, drugs, sex, masturbation. But Jesus sent His Holy Spirit to be our true
comforter.

Let's allow Him to be the comfort in our lives. We
may feel lonely, anxious, or pained, but if we ask
Him to console us, to embrace us, to comfort us, He
will.

*Dear Lord, help me to accept Your comfort so that I in turn may
comfort others.*

> *There is a friend who sticks closer than*
> *a brother.*
> Proverbs 18:24

A British publication once offered a prize for the best definition of a friend. The winning entry read: *A friend is the one who comes in when the whole world has gone out.* As Christians, we know that God is a true friend. He will never leave us or forsake us; He is always "in" regardless of where the rest of the world is.

But what kind of friends are we to Him? Do we turn to Him only when we need His help? He is always there for us in our afflictions. He is also there for us when we are not afflicted to share the good times with us. What kind of friends are we if we call on Him only when we need His help?

God created us that we might worship Him. Let's be true friends to God and spend time with Him daily in fellowship and worship.

Father, help me to grow in maturity, that I may be a friend to You and truly appreciate the kind of friend You are to me.

*For whoever desires to save his life will lose it,
and whoever loses his life for My sake will
find it.*
                                           Matthew 16:25

Before Christ became the center of my life I
thought I was losing everything. I imagined a giant
whirlpool with my husband, children, and home
swirling around me in it. If I could only reach them I
would be saved. They were my life preservers. But,
in spite of my struggling, the force pulling me down
was too great. I could not reach them.

Finally I gave up. I gave it all to the Lord, realizing
I was completely helpless. And at that moment the
picture changed. I was no longer being sucked
down; instead, I was walking on the water toward
Jesus. His hands were outstretched and His eyes
were shining with overwhelming love. My husband,
children, and home were quietly floating around
me within easy reach, if I wanted them. But I no
longer had to have them to survive! Christ was all I
had to have.

Who or what is your life preserver? Have you
found your life in Christ?

Father, help me let go of my life and find Yours.

> *Before I was afflicted I went astray,*
> *But now I keep Your word.*
>
> Psalm 119:67

It was devastating to realize that my abuse was the consequence of my own sin.

As a rebellious young woman I decided to do things my way. I knew what I wanted and I was determined to get it. But, unfortunately, I got much more than I expected.

I married the young man of my choosing. He seemed normal and nice enough—until the wedding vows were spoken. Then I found myself married to a stranger. I was confused, terrified, and trapped. His dark side dominated our lives.

I paid a heavy price for my rebellion. It took years for me to understand what happened. The lessons were painful, but through them I learned to keep God's Word.

Father, I repent of my stiff-necked rebellion. It was hard to be afflicted, but now I know the only way to live is by keeping Your Word.

Let all bitterness, wrath, anger, clamor, and evil speaking be put away from you, with all malice. And be kind to one another, tender-hearted, forgiving one another, just as God in Christ also forgave you.   Ephesians 4:31–32

Writing letters was a major part of my recovery from victimization. Some got mailed; some did not. Just being able to express long-repressed feelings was therapeutic for me.

It felt good saying things I had longed to say, not worrying about how I said them or how the person received them, just getting it all out. To my abuser I wrote of my pain, my anger, and his stain on my life. To the ones who hadn't believed me, I wrote of my devastation and bitter hurt.

Amazingly, as I freely poured forth my resentment and wrath, I felt different. I began to see each person with pity and compassion as through God's eyes. I forgave them, something I had not meant to do.

———————

Thank You, Lord, for giving me a way to get rid of all my pain and to be able to forgive.

His banner over me was love.
Song of Solomon 2:4

A very large flag gently flowed outward from the tall pole, presenting a majestic and inspiring picture. Upon closer inspection the frayed edges of its stripes could be seen, a result of exposure to battering winds. It had seen much use in turbulent weather. But this seemed to add to, rather than detract from, its beauty.

Sexual, emotional, and physical abuse batter our spirits in the same way. We become frayed and wounded. But, as the wounds heal and become scars, they display to the world a certain majesty and inspiration. They become a banner that encourages others to seek healing. God does not erase our wounds so that no one knows they were ever there. He just makes the scars beautiful to behold, His banner of love.

Lord, help me display Your banner in all its glory.

What is hidden he brings forth to light.
Job 28:11

Someone gave me a sexual abuse fact sheet at a retreat. As I read it I found myself all over that sheet of paper—low self-esteem, repeated victimization, self-abuse, and a critical spirit. Could it be? The thought had never occurred to me that I had been abused and that it caused me the problems I was experiencing.

It's like this for many abused women. We don't fully realize what is hidden and how it affects us. But God brings to light the hidden things and frees us from their power. We need only trust His timing and ways.

Thank You, Lord, for bringing to light what is hidden. I trust Your timing and Your ways.

> One thing I have desired of the LORD,
> That will I seek:
> That I may dwell in the house of the LORD
> All the days of my life,
> To behold the beauty of the LORD,
> And to inquire in His temple.

Psalm 27:4

We often waste years of our lives praying for God to bless us with things we badly want. God yearns to bless us, but He does it His way. We don't understand His way, so not recognizing His blessings, we cling to our pitiful desires.

We are finally capable of receiving abundant blessing after we come to the place where we love Him first and desire nothing else. He may then give us those things for which we once so passionately prayed, but the focus of our passion changes and so do our desires. Those things will seem like distractions, even intrusions, for next to life with our beautiful Lord, everything else pales in comparison.

Beautiful Savior, You and You alone are my desire.

*Therefore if the Son makes you free, you shall
be free indeed.*   John 8:36

Advertising portrays seasonal holidays as times of
family fun and merrymaking, but statistics show
that they are times of increased depression and
thoughts of suicide for survivors of dysfunctional
families. Unrealistic expectations based on media
stories and advertising rob us of the true riches of
these holidays. The seasons are meant to be times
of reflection on the goodness of our God and the
love we feel for Him, family, and friends. Instead
they become times of rushing, unfulfilling activity
and expense that for many of us is beyond our
means.

Jesus came to set us free from the hindrances that
rob us of joy. Let us lay aside activities that do not
reflect His goodness and celebrate the true riches of
the Lord this holiday season.

*Jesus, You have set me free. Help me celebrate Your goodness this
season in a way that honors You.*

> *For there is born to you this day in the city of David a Savior, who is Christ the Lord.*
>
> Luke 2:11

Many of us approach Christmas with mixed emotions at the thought of seeing again those family members who filled our past Christmases with pain and anxiety. Apprehension overwhelms us and thoughts of the Babe in the manger get lost in our fear.

Christmas is a season of promises. The angels proclaimed that great joy would be ours because of Christ's birth, and the prophet Isaiah assured us long before that we would call Him *Wonderful!* A gift of hope from our Father above to a world full of hurting people, Jesus was born for healing, deliverance, and joy!

This Christmas, let us put aside all bad memories and focus on the good tidings of the Christ Child. He gives us hope, which says "The best is yet to come!"

I rejoice in Your birth, Lord Jesus, the promise of my hope.

I will give you rest.
Matthew 11:28

It was 2:00 A.M. and the highway was empty. Pressing the accelerator, I steered the car toward an immovable object. There was no fear, no emotion, just the sure knowledge that I wanted to do this. I would have no more pain, only peace and everlasting rest.

I longed to rest in the warmth of another's strength, to taste the sweet nourishment of motherly love, to trust, to live with purpose and confidence. But never in all my twenty years had there been a nurturing touch. My despair was complete.

Then, in my final moments, the feel of God's hand on mine was unmistakable. The steering wheel turned ever so slightly, and my car flew past the object I'd intended to use for my destruction. The car sped through an intersection and careened down the road until, exhausted, I pulled off on a quiet side-street. For the first time since I had vowed as a child that my father would never hurt me again, I wept.

Sometimes it takes the complete exhaustion of final despair for us to discover relief and rest in the Lord.

Thank You, Jesus, that resting in You satisfies all my longings.

> *Bless the Lord, O my soul,*
> *And forget not all His benefits.*
> Psalm 103:2

Holidays can be painful and difficult. We can turn them into times of celebration by focusing on the blessings of the Lord.

New Year's: We have a new beginning, another year of life in Him.

Valentine's Day: We receive endless, unconditional love from Him.

Easter Sunday: We have eternal life and the hope of resurrection.

Memorial Day: God will never leave us or forsake us.

4th of July: We are free from all oppression and bondage because of His blood.

Labor Day: We can cease our labors and enter into His rest.

Thanksgiving: He has provided us with a harvest of blessings.

Christmas: We have the ultimate blessing—the birth of Jesus Christ our Lord.

From beginning to end, the year's holidays become times of celebration, reminders of our good and gracious Father.

Bless the Lord, O my soul, and forget not all His benefits!

*May He grant you according to
your heart's desire,
And fulfill all your purpose.*
Psalm 20:4

After months of feeling fine, I began to be very emotional. I caught myself feeling angry and being critical. Once again male bashing became my favorite pastime. I couldn't figure out what was happening. Why all of these feelings again?

Then I began having migraines, followed by odd physical aches and pains. None of it made sense until the flashbacks began again. In my disappointment and pain, I cried out to God, "Lord, I thought this was over. I thought it was done!"

As I picked up my Bible Psalm 20:4 spoke to me and I realized the Lord will fulfill His purpose for me. I knew then that God will continue revealing and healing those hidden things that keep me from being the person He created me to be.

Please, Lord, continue to fulfill Your purposes for me. Thank You, Lord, for Your faithfulness to me.

> *And Abraham called the name of the place,*
> *The-Lord-Will-Provide.*
>
> Genesis 22:14

Abraham found himself facing the ultimate test of his faith. His entire relationship with God was on the line. Without any evidence of provision, Abraham confessed his belief that God would indeed provide, and God was faithful. As a memorial, Abraham built an altar and called that place *Jehovah-jireh*, "The-Lord-Will-Provide."

We know that Jesus Christ was the lamb provided by God as the ultimate sacrifice for sin. Through Him God made provision for all men. It is written: "Jesus Christ is the same yesterday, today, and forever" (Heb. 13:8). Therefore, God's provision has no end and continues to us today.

When we face ultimate tests we too can experience the place called Jehovah-jireh. If we hold fast to our faith as Abraham did, the Lord will provide. He will perfect everything that concerns us, supplying for every need according to His riches in glory (see Ps. 138:8; Phil. 4:19).

Father, give me the faith to believe that You will be Jehovah-jireh to me.

He has made everything beautiful in its time.
Ecclesiastes 3:11

People say that time is a great healer, that it heals all wounds. We know that time does not heal wounds of the heart; only Jesus Christ can heal those wounds. In His infinite love and wisdom He has a plan of healing for each of us.

While the abuse we have suffered will never be beautiful in anyone's sight, we who have been abused can be beautiful examples of Jesus' healing. While the pain we endured will never be without its price, He can use it to make testimonies to Himself. Though we may bear the scars of abuse throughout our lives, they will always bear witness to the delivering power of our loving Savior.

Our times are in His hands (see Ps. 31:15), and He has appointed a time for every purpose under heaven (see Eccl. 3:1). In His plan for each of us, in time He will make all things beautiful.

Lord, give me eyes to see the beautiful work You are doing in me.

The LORD bless you and keep you;
The LORD make His face shine
  upon you,
And be gracious to you;
The LORD lift up His countenance
  upon you,
And give you peace.

Numbers 6:24–26

As the year comes to a close, let us reflect on the blessings God has given us.

We have been blessed by His very presence and kept in the comfort of His abiding Spirit. We have experienced the warmth of His approving smile. His peace has calmed our minds and soothed our souls. He has shone His light in our darkness. He has graciously comforted us and faithfully encouraged us to go on. We have truly enjoyed the pureness of His love.

Lord, we thank You for bringing us through another year. And with grateful hearts we claim Your promise to abide with us in all things through the new year just beginning. We praise You for Your goodness to us, and in joyful chorus we proclaim:

Blessed be the name of the Lord!
Who has blessed us and kept us,
Who has made His face to shine upon us,
Who has been gracious to us.
Blessed be the name of the Lord!
Who turns not His face from us,
And Who gives us His peace.
Blessed be the name of the Lord!

Many abused women need professional help to work through the relational and personal issues that have surfaced. Many professional agencies and competent individuals are available in various areas of the country. And some churches offer free counseling by trained pastoral staff members and volunteers as well.

If you contact someone for counseling, be sure to evaluate on your own whether you will be comfortable with his or her counsel. Not every counselor knows how God heals sexual abuse. Ask those you contact questions about their methods of treatment, knowledge of your problem, and spiritual orientation before you schedule an appointment. Most counselors will be happy to share their views with you.

Our counseling agency maintains a partial listing of referral sources for different parts of the country. We also provide services for a wide range of problems from sexual abuse to eating disorders, codependency and adolescent problems. If we can be of assistance to you call or write:

Samaritan Counseling Services
8010 E. McDowell Road, Suite B-212
Scottsdale, Arizona 85257
(602) 941-1545

**Library of Congress
Cataloging-in-Publication-Data**

A New beginning / daily devotions for women
   survivors of sexual abuse / Samaritan Counseling
   Center.
        p.   c.m. — (Serenity meditation series)
   ISBN 0-8407-3413-1
   1. Adult child sexual abuse victims—Prayer-books
and devotions—English.   2. Women—Prayer-books
and devotions—English.   3. Devotional calendars.
I. Samaritan Counseling Center.   II. Series.
BV4596.A25N49   1992
242'.643—dc20   92–4042
                                                   CIP